Hustle Endorsements

"In her passionate and moving book, Darieth shares a powerful testimony about how she was able to stay focused on achieving her dreams in the face of adversity, and she encourages each of us to dig deep and tap into our unique gifts to live a better life. Darieth clearly outlines a road map to success and encourages you to not be distracted by the negative or disappointing challenges. Instead she offers a solid plan for building wealth and happiness in simple and realistic ways that will encourage you to get off your butt and make something happen."

Robin Beckham
Founder /Editor
PittsburghUrbanMedia.com
Beckham Media

"Darieth nails it. The courage and commitment that changed her life forever is now a roadmap for others to follow to transform and improve their lives.

Hustle! Is a handbook for success. Darieth delivers the perfect balance of inspiration and real-world action plans.

It's a must read for those who want to ignite a new level of self discovery and for those who want to re-ignite the passion in their lives."

Philip L. Elias
President & CEO
VELOCITY World Media
Elias |Savion

"What a clear provocation: "When you give up on your passions...you put the laws of the universe on hold." You should feel a little uncomfortable reading this book—it's the truth, the laws of the universe, starting to stir and come alive. Darieth connects the impossible not only with the possible...but the probable!"

Darryl Ford Williams
Vice President
of Content for WQED Pittsburgh

"I can't put your book down Darieth! This book is more than just about "Hustle" but is soul stirring and grabs the very essence of one's unadulterated purpose in life. It is a confirmation of what anyone can accomplish with forward thinking, well-defined and focused goals, and the willpower and heart to *Hustle*.

Alice Williams
Women Empowered for Entrepreneurial Excellence
Life and Business Coach

HUSTLE

Why **NOW** is the Time to Unleash Your Passions

- Bonus Materials -
- Hustle Hacks & Action Plans -

DARIETH CHISOLM

ELLECHOR MEDIA

ELLECHOR MEDIA
www.ellechormedia.com

DEDICATION & ACKNOWLEDGEMENT

To Tre, my beautiful and incredible son - thank you for gifting me with motherhood. Thank you for reminding me to be my very best…because someone is watching. Thank you for teaching me the meaning of unconditional love and giving me the opportunity to share it with you and the world. I love you tremendously and it's because of you that the series of events that unfolded in my life gave birth to this book. You are making a significant impact in the world and I'm so proud of you.

To Deborah, my loving and supportive mother - you are my rock, my first architect in life, my princess in the corner. Thank you for always believing in me, for pushing me and for encouraging me to always search my heart and soul and invite spirit and abundance in. I love you and admire you.

To Arnold - I'm grateful for all that we have experienced together. You have been a sounding board, chief of reason and my confidant. Thank you for always supporting me, for listening, for caring, for sharing and for giving me the space, time and freedom to be me. I love you and respect you and all that you are. You are a tremendously gifted doctor, a wonderfully loving father, son, and friend.

To my family, especially my sisters, Traci and Michelle, my brothers Damon, Rajahn and Lacy - we've all been through a lot and through it all we are best friends and a family who shares a beautiful past, weaved together in the most unlikely circumstances. Still our love and families continue to grow. Thank you for your love, support, belief and guidance.

To my friends....your Girl did it! I thank you all for your love, support, kind words and encouragement. So many of you have played a significant role in who I am today and I'm grateful for our journey together. This book is for you. Hustle! Hustle like today is all you have, because there is no better time than Now.

CONTENTS

Introduction

Hustle is the never ending flow of energy and commitment that sets the extremely successful people apart from the majority. Successful entrepreneurs hustle like there's no tomorrow. At every attempt, they give it their all, all of their attention, focus, energy, and commitment. Hustlers are not afraid to fail, they're not afraid to go after what they want in spite of their doubts or the naysayers, they simply remain in action working and enjoying their journey. Hustling is about taking action before the perfect conditions arise, taking a leap of faith before we receive permission, stepping out before it appears reasonable, and moving forward before others anticipate your next move.

-Darieth Chisolm-

Most of us are working hard on the proverbial treadmill of life, whacking away at accomplishing some dream or task, completing some to do list, or firing daily at a goal that seems to elude us. This point was brought glaringly home to me on one of my recent business trips.

My travel schedule is usually hectic and insane. I'm 5'11", and squeezing into the airplane restroom is a challenge, so once the plane lands, I generally find myself eager to make it to a real bathroom. A few months ago, I scurried off a plane with my knees knocking, anxious to get to the toilet, only to find myself standing in a long line.

As I stood waiting, all I could hear on the other side of the wall was a woman with a thick accent saying, "Welcome to the clean ladies restroom. Have a great day!"

When I made my way around the corner, I could finally see the face of the woman who was singing this broken phrase. She was busy trying to manage the cleanliness of each stall and the small area where she had put some toiletries, paper towels, and feminine products, along with candies and mints.

Then I noticed a jar filled with a few quarters and a couple of dollars sitting next to her display. I glanced up at her and caught a glimpse of sweat rolling down her face as she raced over to hand a paper towel to a person who was about to tip her. She then retrieved the dirty paper towel and shoved it into her front pocket. Her melodic chant started again: "Welcome to the clean ladies restroom. Have a great day!"

I started thinking about how long she's been doing this. Is she here all the time, busy servicing hurried passengers who are in a haste to catch their next flight? Does she love what she's doing? Is this what she imagined herself becoming when she was a young girl?

She was definitely hustling and working hard, but was it paying off?

Was this what she wanted to be doing in life?

Was she really passionate about wiping dirty toilet seats for mere quarters?

What if she could take the same energy, same commitment, same work ethic, and hustle and unleash it into her own dream?

What if she could develop a business, product, or service? What if she could excel and become successful promoting or selling someone else's product or service?

Don't get me wrong, her service was needed and much appreciated, at least by those of us who realize the toil and customer service involved in wiping toilets every three seconds.

But is that all there is for her and millions of others who are not challenging themselves or their circumstances to live a greater, more joyful and fulfilled life?

If I could put my arms around her, give her a hug, and ensure her, from the bottom of my heart, that she could be more, do more, and deserves more, then I would. But that was for another time and place, because that opportunity is no longer available.

Instead, I get an opportunity to do that with you. I want my words to wrap around your soul, and encourage you to step away from your past and limiting beliefs and step up to a greater you and a greater future.

However desperate your life may seem, there is always hope and opportunity for change. No matter how bad the circumstances appear, there are better days ahead. You can rise above whatever challenges you may be experiencing and unleash your passion, despite the circumstances that might be suggesting otherwise. You are greater than those challenges. You are bigger than those circumstances. It simply starts with deciding to take action now and focus on something positive. Take advantage of whatever light exists in your life right now and shine it squarely on what is really important to you and then start working for a better outcome.

Too often we tell ourselves we aren't smart enough or attractive enough or talented enough to pursue our passions. We listen to what others say about us, and we put restrictions on our talents and our capabilities. We listen to those voices and, what's even worse, add our own inner dialogue to the choir bellowing out messages of unworthiness.

We feel unprepared and ill-equipped. We start putting limits on what we can be, on what we can do, and on what we can have, eventually stopping the free flowing process of creation. I know—I have done this too many times to count.

This book is about letting go of those self-limiting, self-doubting beliefs and habits. It's about stopping the self-sabotage we inflict on ourselves around our own abilities and potential.

This book is especially for you, if you are finally ready to move past the doubts and fears you've allowed to block you. If you are prepared to dig deeper to find greater purpose and meaning in your work, business, hobbies, or projects, I am here to guide the way. Together we will do the needed work of rising to the occasion, exposing your truths, and bringing your greatness to the surface.

We will decide and declare, unapologetically, to unleash our passions! In so doing, you will attract the wealth and abundance, money and connections, peace and joy that go with living a life in high energy.

Entrepreneurs are so busy wearing so many hats and doing so many things that they often lose focus on *why* they are in business in the first place. Often, the passion has long since left the building, and what's left is an empty shell of a frazzled, overworked, and exhausted dreamer.

I proclaim that we will stop this draining cycle and renew you with the spirit of your passion, refueling you for the journey ahead.

But before we dive in, let's look at where most of us are before we discover our purpose.

As an award-winning television news anchor, a serial entrepreneur, video podcast host, speaker, author, and success coach, I am still exploring new horizons and pursuing new passions. I have learned from my journey that it is when you are not focused on what makes you happy that the pursuit which makes you tick and fires you into your "zone" will tend to fizzle. When you don't feel your passion oozing from every pore as you think and talk about what gets you going, then you are missing the magic that makes dreams a reality.

When you give up on your passions and your dreams, or dismiss them as whimsical adventures, you put the laws of the universe on hold.

You have choices. You can choose to be handicapped by the results of those choices. You can dwell on the disappointments and shortcomings thrown in your path. You can choose to be bitter, sad, and angry about what is happening around you. You can also focus on hard times and hurtful people and, thereby, choose the damaging results associated with these choices.

Or…

You can take responsibility for those experiences and learn from them. You can take the next step, move forward, and make bigger and better plans. You can focus on something positive and choose to harness what God has given you and share it with the world.

If you are in business for yourself, an entrepreneur, or thinking about starting a business, you are likely fueled by an insatiable desire to be successful and enjoy the riches of your blood, sweat, and tears. No doubt the people in *my life* would label me as a hard worker, a big dreamer, and a hustler. I am also a huge believer, and one of my greatest passions is believing in others.

In this book I will share rituals, principles, hacks, and strategies that I have found most successful entrepreneurs practice and believe in—ten areas of your life that, when improved upon with desire and passion, can help you produce great results. I will also introduce you to several successful entrepreneurs who have used these same strategies.

I will give you concrete action steps that will help you map out your next move. I will share real life experiences of others just like you. My years of experience enable me to share tried and true advice, real tactics, and practical solutions to help you hustle in pursuit of your passions, with a dose of encouragement along the way. We'll talk about fears and doubts and how to move past them and how to overcome the challenges that are stopping you from pursuing your dreams. We will look at identifying how to use hardships as opportunities to discover who you are—and who you are meant to be—allowing you to share your gifts and talents to benefit others.

I truly believe that if you have the passion and the inner motivation to do or have something, you will achieve it. But you're going to need a few things along the way. Below are my "10 Rituals of Highly Successful Entrepreneurs." If we can all agree with the Merriam Webster definition of "ritual," it is an act or series of acts done in a particular situation and in the same way each time. By all means, this list is not complete, but it is certainly verifiable by the numbers of people who have achieved what they are dreaming of by using and practicing these techniques. Go through this list and ask yourself these questions:

Darieth's 10 Rituals of Highly Successful Entrepreneurs

Are you...?
A Courageous Spirit?
Hungry for Opportunity?
Authentically and Unapologetically You?
Fearless and Brave?

Do you have...?
A Powerful Sense of Purpose?
Love and Self-Acceptance?
Abundance and Flow?
Defined Action Plans?
A Mission to Serve Others?
Hustle?

Then you are ready to go!
I believe these rituals are the fundamentals needed for unleashing your passions, turning them into profit, and loving your journey along the way.

You'll get a chance to read excerpts of guest interviews from my video podcast show *Hustle & Heart TV*. I will share key Hustle & Heart tips from these business experts, illustrating how to find your own never-ending flow of energy and commitment—your hustle—and do what you love—your heart. When you want more highlights and inspiration from those guests, you can turn to their episodes on HustleandHeartTV.com and watch their entire message or go to the Resource section in the back of the book to take advantage of our 14 Day Plan.

I set out to write this book with the intent to encourage entrepreneurs to be steadfast and unwavering in their commitment to achieving success with their business, to overcome their challenges and hardships, and to stop allowing these things to block their blessings. I will help you find your own purpose and discover the pathways to turning your new endeavors into the life you've always dreamed of.

My aim is to inspire others to move with faith, hope, love, and belief that dreams do come true, and with hustle and heart yours can too. I pray that I'll light the path to a place where you'll discover a stronger you, a bolder you, a more determined and more empowered you. It is time to unleash your passion and pursue the life you were meant to lead. It is possible! And together, we can make it happen!

CHAPTER ONE

A COURAGEOUS SPIRIT

There is No Better Time than Now

There is a plane of awareness that you can opt to live at, wherein you can, if you are willing to change your concept of yourself as an ordinary being, find yourself fulfilling any and all wishes that you have for yourself.

-Dr. Wayne Dyer-

How many of you were told when you were growing up that you could be anything you wanted? That you could do anything you set your mind to? That you could accomplish whatever your heart desired? My mother and grandmother used to tell me these things all the time, so I grew up believing nothing was impossible.

But I still carried tons of doubt. I was this chubby, little girl who had low self-esteem and weight issues. My father was absent, living thousands of miles away in Charleston, South Carolina, and had been paralyzed from the waist down after he was shot when I was just two years old. However, I still firmly believed in fairy tales, princesses, storybook endings, and limitless opportunities. I played with my "baby dolls" and imagined happily-ever-after endings for their lives all the way up until the age of twelve. I know that's a bit old, but with my dolls I could dream and have conversations and go places with my imaginary friends that the neighborhood girls just weren't up for.

When I was younger, I had no idea I was living in poverty. We were poor and broke, and my mother, as a single young woman, was constantly struggling just to pay the rent and utilities and care for me and my brother.

"It didn't have to be that tough!" I would imagine my grandfather telling my mom. You see, she walked away from a track scholarship at the age of eighteen when she became pregnant with me. Even though my supportive grandparents offered to raise me while my mother went back to school, my mom struggled with quitting the team, knowing this meant giving up on her only chance of attending college. Ultimately, her passion to become a good mother far outweighed her desire to run track, and she returned home to marry my dad, an older suave gentleman. Shortly after my birth she became pregnant with my brother. She was now the mother of two children at the age of nineteen. My mother and father separated before the birth of my brother. Two years later, my father was shot several times in the back, which left him paralyzed from the waist down. I can't imagine how my mother handled two young children, an estranged paralyzed husband, and no money. My parents divorced shortly after the accident, and my memories of my father are few. The times I can remember were mostly from his stay at the Veterans Hospital in Detroit, where he was confined to a wheelchair. I did see him a few summers when we would visit him in South Carolina. My father had a previous marriage before he and my mother tied the knot, so I have an older sister and brother, Traci and Lacy, plus a younger sister, Michelle. He later passed away when I was fifteen.

By the time my mother's second marriage ended in divorce, she had given birth to my baby brother Rajahn, and she was now a single mother of three. Needless to say my young life was full of uncertainty. We moved fifteen times before my fourteenth birthday, and not once but twice we lived in houses that didn't have a working refrigerator or a functioning stove. We had to use hotplates and crockpots to cook our meals. The blessing was that one time when the refrigerator didn't work, it was winter, so we could put our food that needed to be refrigerated outside on the back porch.

I remember on a couple of occasions not having hot running water or that the lights were out, and we, like most of my friends at that time, only occasionally had a working phone. Money was always tight or nonexistent. It was not an ideal situation to say the least. We had a three-month stretch when we survived by collecting money from a newspaper route. If you've ever had a paper route, you might remember going to a cold warehouse to roll and stuff the newspapers. You would head out to deliver the newspapers and then collect the money from your customers. My mother, Damon, and I all threw papers one long, cold, snowy, Detroit winter just to make ends meet. I can still smell the ink from the loads of newspapers piled in the back seat and trunk of my mother's station wagon.

That station wagon was an old but trusty set of wheels. I remember before that we always had clunkers on the verge of breaking down. When we did have a running vehicle—and the money to purchase a gallon of gas—a stop at the gas station and just three bucks went along way. We really knew how to stretch a dollar! I remember my mom waving the money in her hand, telling us to get two dollars in gas, pay fifty-five cents for a pack of Salem cigarettes, and my brother and I could have the change. We had forty-five cents to split between us for penny candy and two Faygo Pops. Through it all and as bad as it was, at the time it never really seemed that tough, because we had each other.

Even though there was poverty, despair, and crime outside of our homes in Detroit, it never really impacted me as a child. It wasn't because I wasn't aware of it, but because my mother never let our financial situation negatively scar me. She never, ever complained, and seemed to always have a smile on her face. She was a remarkably beautiful pillar of strength. She was always encouraging us to dream big, and she modeled an unbridled enthusiasm for striving for excellence in everything she did.

We may have lived in shacks and moved around frequently, but we were always sketching out our "beautiful dream home" together as a family on scratch paper. This led to me creating dream and vision boards at a young age. We were constantly thinking about what it would be like to live in an enormous house, with our bedrooms decorated exactly the way we wanted. My mother was always dreaming, so we were always dreaming. She never appeared to let anything hold her back in spite of what we were facing. She loved us, protected us, and provided for us the best way she knew how. She was always our champion, and she was our "dream architect," who always nurtured in us the incentive to build ourselves, build a different life, and build a better tomorrow.

DREAM

I know without a shadow of a doubt that each of us has the power and capacity to build a better tomorrow. We must plant the seeds for a bright future today and draw the plans for tomorrow with a childlike imagination. Your dreams, combined with passion and purpose, create a catalytic power for change.

So how can we do this and be exceptional at work, at home, in our communities, and in life? In the words of Mahatma Gandhi, "Be the change you want to see in the world."

You are talented and gifted in various ways. You are real estate agents, bankers, lawyers, doctors, assistants, teachers, administrators, business owners, civic leaders, mothers, and fathers. You represent the pieces that make the community a healthy and whole puzzle. But are we doing enough? Are we dreaming enough? Can we become more, be more, do more, have more, and serve more?

You know, all those years ago my mother had a grand design and was the architect for the life I'm living today. She was drafting the dream I'm living. Every time we sat down to the kitchen table to sketch out our dream home, we were getting closer to its reality.

I'm a girl who grew up poor and broke in the inner city of Detroit, who moved fifteen times before I was fourteen, who sometimes didn't have heat, water, or a working stove and refrigerator. The drugs, poverty, crime, and hopelessness that were surrounding me growing up could have easily influenced me. But it didn't. It didn't because of my mother, the dream architect. She built me differently. So I went on to build a life that affords me the opportunity to now impact others to build a life of their dreams, and I get to stand on the sidelines and watch them come true.

I'm proud to say my husband and I designed and built our 5,000-square-foot dream home and paid it off within three years. Living debt-free is important to me. I also own another home in Florida. Wealth building and being debt free has been one of my dreams come true.

You see, none of this was possible if I didn't believe in myself and my dreams, and if I didn't hustle for them.

It doesn't matter what your past looks like, it doesn't matter what your present life is—it only matters that you are resolute in creating a better tomorrow for you and your family. You must want your dreams and be willing to fight for them like a drowning man wants air!

Decide to create an extraordinary life. Refuse to play small or to give up. Do not follow the crowd. Choose the road less traveled and walk toward the fulfillment of your dream.

Where there is a will, there is a way, and moving toward that way begins right now. Get ready to unleash your passion and hustle for your dreams. If a little, poor girl, who suffered from poor self-esteem, who had a paralyzed, absent father, and who faced other personal challenges had the courage to realize her dreams, so can you!

In my lifetime, I have worn many hats. I've been an award-winning television news anchor; a serial entrepreneur owning several small businesses; a top network marketing sales leader; a speaker; a business coach; an author; an iTunes #1 rated video podcast show host; and a mom and a wife. Yet after all of that, I still sometimes feel like I'm not living up to my personal best and completely exploring the true depth of my passions. When that warning light appears, I know it's time for change, a change in me or a change in my situation.

You might be like me: at first, I felt isolated and alone when it came to unleashing my passions. I felt I would be judged, ridiculed, and labeled, especially for my desires to start one of those—often mistakenly referred to as—"pyramid schemes" and "MLM" or "network marketing businesses."

Until one day I just decided to jump. I just decided to take a leap of faith and play out, in living color, my dreams as an entrepreneur.

Still, I did it in fits and spurts. I spent twenty years as, what I call, a "peek-a-boo entrepreneur," playing the role of a television news anchor. It was a glorious and successful career as one of three main anchors at the NBC affiliate in Pittsburgh, WPXI Channel 11 News. While I loved my career and all the fanfare and accolades that came with it, my soul always cried out for more. Only through entrepreneurship did I find my passion for creating and growing businesses fulfilled.

I named myself this "peek-a-boo entrepreneur" because I pulled the proverbial mask off every once in a while to expose the "wannabe" entrepreneur who was tucked safely inside. I was protected by a well-paying job and career, so I could afford to start a business here and start a business there and never fully commit as a sole entrepreneur.

My life has been full of starting small businesses, joining network marketing companies, and dreaming up products and ideas. Fortunately many of my ventures were successful, the training ground for perfecting my entrepreneurship skills. Once I allowed myself to dream, nothing was truly impossible for me. It was like when I was a child, immersing myself fully into these fantasy dream spaces that included everything I wanted and needed in life. As a child I dreamed about escaping the poverty and despair; as an adult I dream to create my beautiful results.

I share these stories with you to inspire you to find the courage to take that leap of faith and launch out into the unknown.

The first step in this process is establishing your dream, the impetus for your "why."

Do you dream of creating an extraordinary life? One filled with enough joy, freedom, health, happiness, time, adventure, love, prosperity, and peace? Do you dream of boldly expressing your talents, gifts, and passions? Is it a goal of yours to have a perfect work-life balance where you can spend your time doing what you love and bringing value to others, while enjoying your family and friends? A life where you can't wait to get out of bed each morning to live and share your talent and passions with the world? A life where the world is waiting for you with open arms?

Or are you on a boring roller coaster of ups and downs, bad times, and bad breaks, experiencing a constant nausea because you just can't stand the way things are right now? You hate what's showing up in your life, and it's everybody else's fault.

Here's the deal: whatever your view of your life is, it's *your* interpretation. While you may be facing some very tough times, or you might be enjoying a beautiful, grand expression of paradise, your life is showing up now just the way you see it. Your focus and attention are carving out your future. The pictures in your mind and the emotions in your heart either stir and energize you or drag and pull you down. It's your choice.

CHOICE

It's your choice to believe and act as you see fit. It's your choice to pay attention to what's good or bad in your life. It's your choice to react to it, claim it and embrace it, or ignore and avoid it. Whatever you do, you will live with the outcome. Why not choose now to change?

To achieve a great life, you must be willing to make a great sacrifice. Make up your mind to go for it! Decide to create an extraordinary life. Where there is a will, there is a way. Believe in yourself right now, even though it may be hard. Do not allow yourself to be overwhelmed by darkness, surrounded by negativity, or give into despair. None of these things improve your life. Do not give yourself permission to feel sorry for yourself. Whatever you do, never, never, never give up your personal power.

Start right now to take massive action on your own behalf to move your life forward. You can do this! Keep your mind focused on the outcome you desire. It takes disciplining your mind, heart, and spirit to create your breakthrough. What you think about, you bring about. Despite all of your circumstances and all the challenges you are facing, now is the time for you to believe in yourself.

You were born to do great things. Now is the time to leap over those obstacles of fear, procrastination, and self-doubt. Determine what you really want out of life and go after it!

You may be saying, "Yes, I know this stuff, but I'm still not getting anywhere." I'm fully aware there are several life scenarios that may be influencing your choices. For example a long-term relationship may have ended, and you are devastated, confused, and shocked. You are in pain and feel disillusioned about your future. However, this is the most opportune time to move on. Now is the time for you to recreate something beautiful in your life. Pain often precedes progress and prosperity. Embrace the moment to move toward the good in your life and create something beautiful out of any bad experience.

You may have outgrown certain situations in your life, and you have to find the courage to move on. You may have been told that your job is going in another direction and they are not taking you with it. You've dedicated your whole life to being the best employee an employer could have, and now this happens. You may be an entrepreneur who has always dreamed of having your own restaurant, you took the plunge, and now you are facing foreclosure. Or you may have trusted a good friend's advice on investing in a lucrative business deal, invested your life's savings, and now you are penniless because the deal went south. Your mind is reeling and the fear of financial failure is gripping your heart.

Though devastation can be heart-shattering, at this very moment you must shake it off and move on. Now is the time. Moving on does not mean that you give up; moving on means that no bad relationship, no lost job, no failed business attempt, no financial hardship, or any other thing is worth missing your opportunity for a resurrection. Now is your time to *hustle*.

Do not focus on the things that you have lost. Refocus your mind on what you want your bright future to look like. Get still, go within, and trust that your revolutionary change is occurring. Revise your mental blueprint to look for the good in the midst of this perceived bad situation.

Failure is not a destination. It is an invitation to unforeseen victories. A person who has never failed has never really tried. Make failure your opportunity to try again to get it right. When you fall, especially when it hurts, be willing to pick yourself up, dust yourself off, and get back in the game. You are not competing against anyone, not even yourself. Life is not a sprint—it is a marathon. Are you in it to win it?

Genius, Albert Einstein, had this to say about change: "The world as we have created it is a process of our thinking. It cannot be changed without changing our thinking."

Choose now to change your thinking. Find the courage that has been strategically placed in you by your Creator for such a time as this. Face your fears head on. Embrace each moment that you feel you "blew it." Remember, it is just a memory. The past only exists in your mind. You have the absolute power to release it. There is a fundamental difference between failure and temporary defeat. Be willing to fail your way to success! You have not failed. You have merely graduated into a brand new opportunity to manifest the greatness within you!

DECIDE

You can start over again! Right now! Now is your time to decide and declare that this is your opportunity, your chance, your new start to pursue your passion, live your dream, and live your best life *now*! Now is the time to unleash the very best you that has anxiously been waiting inside of you.

Don't retreat when you don't see the metamorphosis happening fast enough. It is easy to replay in your mind how things did not work, how much you lost, what you are going through, how angry you are. But there is no amount of negative self-talk that is going to wipe the slate clean. You are wasting valuable time and energy that could be used to regain a new normal and start another chapter of your life. Even though you are hurt and you may be feeling down, stop kicking yourself! Face what has happened. Make the decision now to start over again.

In life, friendships change, divorces happen, people move on, loved ones die. Money and jobs will come and go. Don't look back. Look straight ahead! Decide to use all of your knowledge, skills, experiences, life lessons, defeats, and setbacks to start over again. Life changes—learn to embrace the changes. You may not have the same life as before, but you can still enjoy the rest of your life.

Will you wallow in yesterday's accomplishments and failures? I believe that certificates and diplomas should be used as catalysts to inspire you to pursue your next level of success, not as reminders of past achievements. Don't allow yourself to get stuck in yesterday and become complacent about reaching your highest potential for success today.

AVOID HEAD TRASH

Don't be a garbage can for anything that does not feed your intellect, stimulate your imagination, or make you a more compassionate, peaceful person. Refuse to open your mind to other people's trash. Tune out anything that promotes conflict. Continuous struggle can infect you with a virus of cynicism and defeat, and you won't even know it! Its invisible tentacles have the power to hold you captive to the wrong mindset. Free yourself by taking the garbage out and putting a new trash bag in the can. Better yet, throw out the old can and get a new one in honor of your decision to celebrate the new things that are coming your way!

Be deliberate about setting up your day to win. Whatever you feed your mind in the first thirty minutes of the day will impact the spirit of your day. Saturate yourself with positive words that fuel your energy and ignite your spirit. Your thoughts create your reality. Now is the time to start your *new* reality, and the fuel you'll use to propel you forward is your passion. Decide now to unleash your passion and hustle for your dreams. They can be yours! With enough hustle, passion, persistence, and belief, you can start living your dreams and expressing the greatest version of who you want to become.

Have you spent your life making to-do lists that you never end up completing? You may get stuck in that place because you have not made the connection with the other components of the equation for successful goal completion. Get the bigger picture by adding a "to be" and "to have" list. Write down what it is you want to do, what you want to become as a result, and what you want to have at the end of this process. Your rewards can be tangible or intangible. It's more important for you to bring clarity to this process by being specific about what you want to do, who you want to become, and what you want to have at the end of this journey.

A great way to remind yourself daily of your personal "to do," "to be," and "to have" lists is to create a vision board or a dream board. It's also a great way to keep a record of your accomplishments.

I was watching famed comedian Steve Harvey's special, *Act Like a Success, Think Like a Success*, and he shared the importance of keeping your vision board close to you. He has his on his iPhone and iPad as a constant reminder of where he's headed. His goals are to build generational wealth for his family, send ten thousand children to college on full scholarships, and help the continent of Africa build a successful infrastructure. You may think these are huge goals for one man…but nothing is impossible for you when you put a demand on the universe to make a withdrawal from your account of possibilities, and you are willing to hustle to make it happen!

What are you willing to withdraw from your account of possibilities?

ACTION PLAN

Your thoughts equal your desires. You get what you think about, whether you want it or not.

Write your answers to the following questions. Construct a positive confession for each comment. Then read them over several times daily until they become a part of the new you.

EXAMPLE: Question: *What is your immediate response to disappointments?*

Reader's Response: *I usually get angry and pout.*

Positive Confession: *When I am faced with disappointments, I choose to hug myself with this positive affirmation—I still possess the power to allow this to positively change me, not chain me to this disappointment. I activate that power now.*

QUESTIONS

1. Is your constant thought pattern positive or negative?
2. What is your attention focused on more often than not?
3. Is your thinking full of fear and consequently you are attracting negative life opportunities

from a place of inner anxiety, worry, or doubt?

4. Are you thinking grateful thoughts and expressing gratitude for the gifts life has given you?

5. Do you possess a sense of awe for every breath you take and possess a level of positive anticipation for your life?

6. What thoughts are you willing to give up now, in order to get the things you truly desire?

HUSTLE TIP

"You have to make it real and act immediately. As soon as you see it, move forward and act on it."

- Sabrina Saunders, Pittsburgh Executive Director of Strong Women Strong Girls - *Hustle & Heart TV* on Episode 14

HEART TIP

"Make sure that whatever you do stirs your soul."

- Sabrina Saunders, Pittsburgh Executive Director of Strong Women Strong Girls - *Hustle & Heart TV* on Episode 14

CHAPTER TWO

HUNGRY FOR OPPORTUNITY

Your Passion Will Lead the Way

When you trust that you have blessings, talents, knowledge,
love to share with others, you will begin the journey to
self-acceptance, even if your gifts are not yet apparent.
Once you begin that walk, others will find you
and walk with you.

-Nick Vujicic-

Unleashing your passion and being great at what you love doing always gives you the opportunity to live life more fully and freely. Let your light shine brightly; let those things that you love doing and love being guide you in the direction of your greatest achievements.

We must awaken each day with clarity and purpose foremost on our minds, centered directly on our passions. Then and only then will we trust that this is a deeply momentous time in our lives for change and growth.

We could choose to be a coward, standing before our passions, wishing for the perfect circumstances to allow us to finally unleash them. *You* hold the key to unleashing your passions. When will you release that greatness that is stirring inside of you? Grab hold of your deepest desires and ride them relentlessly until you get what you are asking for!

Our passions fuel us; they give us the inherent insight to lead us to greater levels of joy, fulfillment, and happiness. When we are strongly engrossed in doing what we are passionate about, we enter a zone, a place of being that seems limitless and bountiful and comes with an internal sense of well-being. When we turn this sense of well-being loose into the world, great things happen.

Think of all the accomplishments and achievements that can unfold when a person unleashes their passion. The author of our quote, Nicholas James "Nick" Vujicic, is an Australian Christian evangelist and motivational speaker born with tetra-amelia syndrome. Nick has no limbs—no arms or legs—yet he travels more than most, crossing the world, sharing his message of hope and triumph. His passion is evangelism and empowering people to do the seemingly impossible. He is a living testimony of not allowing your limits to dictate how you master the opportunities that come your way.

Think of the times when you were so passionately charged that you felt unstoppable, unshakeable, and fearless when working toward a goal. It goes without saying—no accomplishment is achieved without passion.

In spite of growing up poor, I still had a strong desire to go to college. My mother and I weren't sure how we were going to pay for it, but I stayed focused on my passion for journalism, and I sought out countless ways to get a college scholarship.

I started in the tenth grade, way too early to apply, but I was resolute on attending college. Fortunately, it happened; I received a scholarship to attend Wayne State University.

However, it only covered my tuition. I knew I would need to make extra money to cover other costs. My entrepreneur's sixth sense started to tingle, so I started a vending machine service company at nineteen. I called it "Prelude Services," somehow knowing it was the start to something big. It was a flashback to when I was even younger, a little girl of eight who was passion-driven and focused on the success of her "Bam Bam's Juicy Juice Stand." But Prelude Services was clearly more serious. I got a bank account, EIN number, business cards, secured thirteen locations, and began loading cans of pop into my beat-up Chevy Horizon. With the help of my supportive family, it was a huge success, providing me with several hundred extra dollars a month and a huge sense of accomplishment.

My passion for entrepreneurship was also fueled by my distinct ability to create an idea, bring it to market, and then watch it grow and expand. These desires had been cultivating in my heart for years, and I knew they provided me with the fuel to ignite my dreams and to get out there and make things happen.

There were times, though, when I was just too afraid to let the flame fully burn. Is that where you are, afraid to light that inner fire that gets you motivated and moving? Keep reading—there are a few "matches" on the pages to come that will help you "light your fire."

Remember, it's that inner flame that keeps us hustling, and we always need to find ways to stoke the fire, because when the passion dies, the business dies. I know this—I've been there, too.

So let me ask you: what are you waiting on to unleash your passion?

I hope it's not perfection.

PERFECTION

Waiting on perfection is such a time waster. Trying to make things perfect is pointless. Perfection rarely happens, and while you pour over the details, trying to make something perfect, those powerful thoughts about what you can create and who you can become fall helplessly away from your mind.

Stop waiting on perfecting your passion to open your treasure trove of possibilities. If you wait, you will never fully explore the greatest expression of who you truly are, and all of the missed opportunities of sharing your gifts and talents will be wasted as you hide behind the allure of perfection.

Being great at unleashing your passion has nothing to do with being perfect. Get over it; you may as well stop holding yourself back, waiting on the perfect outcome, time, situation, or conclusion to move forward. Perfection simply doesn't exist. No one is perfect, and believing otherwise is what stops some people from striving for greatness. They mistakenly associate successful people with perfection, thereby missing the opportunity to expose their own greatest gifts.

Here's the truth: Successful people simply do what unsuccessful people don't do or are unwilling to do. Successful people are usually driven by their passion and show up and do the work, over and over again, with little care about being perfect. What successful people generally know is that they will get better, be great, and get close to being perfect by doing what they are passionate about, repeatedly. In my experience I have found that the secret to getting close to being perfect at something is to do it consistently and never give up. It is a repetitive process that only time can accomplish. Working at perfecting what you love to do is priceless.

POTENTIAL

So now that we've lightened the load and dismissed our thoughts about being perfect, let's look at potential. Potential is a *big* word that usually refers to latent qualities or abilities that may be developed and could lead to future success or usefulness. We all have potential—the question is are you using and leveraging yours?

Most people never realize their potential because they do not trust that their passion is the sole ingredient to igniting that potential. The beliefs that you hold about yourself in relationship to your skills and abilities generally determines your potential. Our beliefs act as a framework for our behavior. In other words what you believe forms the cornerstone of how you behave and whether or not you use your potential.

Engaging your potential may require you to develop a way of thinking that will help you to believe you can behave differently. Just because you may have failed in the past doesn't mean you will fail again. If you really want to change something in your life, know that if you truly believe it can happen, then you will find a way to make it happen.

Belief fuels your potential, and passion drives your outcome. If you are attempting to do anything new or remotely ambitious in your life, like start a new business, end an old relationship, take charge of your health, or launch into a new adventure, check in with your overall belief system to ensure that you are congruent. When you believe you can achieve great things, you will.

It is also worth pointing out that one of the functions performed by our mind is the validation of our way of thinking about the world. We will tend to seek confirmation for what we believe, even if those beliefs are harmful to our well-being. If you believe that you are capable and confident, you pay attention to those signals from the outside world that reinforce those beliefs. If you believe that you are not as good as others or that you are being judged badly, you also readily seek that confirming evidence. When this happens, often at the first sign of difficulty in achieving an objective, you are more likely to leave your plans and shrink back into your comfort zone, abandoning your potential and losing your passion.

You may need to create space for a new belief system and let some old beliefs and habits go before they wreck your potential for a new life. If not, they will destroy your passion, prohibiting you from setting sail for new opportunities in your life.

There is nothing more powerful than being able to recreate yourself while you are moving through a life-changing transition. A new opportunity, fueled by your passion and leveraged by your potential, provides you with a fresh start. When you are granted a fresh chance to get it right a second or even third time around, be careful not to blow the new opportunities with old beliefs.

I've seen many people at the top of their vocation consistently foster their limitless potential. They don't believe they are perfect, they simply believe they cannot fail. They believe in their potential. This unwavering belief in themselves allows them to be better than they really are. The more successful they become, the more evidence appears to support their belief in their own greatness. We have the power and ability within ourselves to be, do, have, and become any number of things in our pursuit of greatness.

So how can we achieve excellence and become exceptional in business? Establish the following principles and be consistent in your use of them when building a successful future.

PRINCIPLES

My years of interviewing many successful people enable me to share some key principles that most successful people practice. Fortunately, success can be yours too when you utilize principles that rarely fail those who use them wisely. These proven principles are foolproof. No matter the area of expertise required, success is inevitable when these philosophies are implemented. Much of this is not foreign to you; you probably already have repeated some of these statements to yourself. You may stare at them as pieces of artwork in your office, digest them in your car, listen to a favorite podcast, or speak them to your children. Principles like:

- Set goals and work really hard for them!
- Never give up and always believe in yourself.
- The Golden Rule: do unto others as you would have them do unto you.
- It's not what you know but who you know.
- You can do anything you put your mind to.

I could go on and on, right?

ACTION PLAN

When you establish principles that are in line with your passion and your potential, then you escape the trap of trying to be perfect. You are free to unleash your greatest results.

Write your answers to the following questions. Construct a positive confession for each comment, then read them over several times daily, until they become a part of the new you.

EXAMPLE:

Question: *In what way does your passion fuel your dreams?*

Response: *When I am looking for the energy to start a project, I test myself to see if I am experiencing a high level of excitement.*

Positive Confession: *When my passion is activated, I am elevated and accelerated to complete the task at hand. I choose to activate my passion now.*

QUESTIONS

1. What are you most passionate about?
2. What gives you the greatest amount of joy?

3. What have you put aside while waiting for perfection that you could put into action now, as is?
4. What potential are you not fully exploring?
5. What principles have you set for your life?

If you're still trying to figure out what you're passionate about or you need to clearly define it, start with asking yourself a few questions to help direct you toward your goals:

- What do you love doing that you can offer others that will fulfill their needs?
- What are you talented or skilled at that can be of service to others?

HUSTLE TIP

"Going into it prepared, there are a number of aspects to it. Do you have a brand? Do you have a concept? Have you tested it? Have you worked with it before opening? Being prepared is very important; being capitalized, not going into it on a string. You've got to have the ability to get through a rough time... if your opening is slow or if things aren't going quite right. As soon as you start struggling for those dollars, you start giving up things that you should not give up, whether it be your payroll or your quality or those sorts of things. Just be very well prepared for that and making sure you like what you do, and you have people that like their jobs."

- Pat McDonnell, CEO of Restaurant Holdings: Atria's, Juniper Grill and Ditka's – *Hustle & Heart TV* on Episode 13

HEART TIP

"Heart is truly what it's about. We [at *Restaurant Holdings*] have a principle called 'value of the person,' and it's a subject. It's a company that my wife founded with her father about 40 years ago. It's about love, dignity, and respect. We try to live by those principles of love, dignity, and respect, to build relationships at the workplace and at home with your kids, with your spouse, with your family, and it really, really works, so we preach that."

- Pat McDonnell, CEO of Restaurant Holdings: Atria's, Juniper Grill and Ditka's – *Hustle & Heart TV* on Episode 13

CHAPTER THREE

AUTHENTICALLY AND UNAPOLOGETICALLY YOU

Take the Mask Off

Forget those things which are behind and reach for
the things that are ahead. Leave your cocoon
and spread your wings!

-T.D. Jakes-

M y entrepreneur journey is so diverse, with lots of ups and downs and twists and turns. It appears that my path is much like many other business owners: a plethora of win some, lose some. Like most others, I am spurred on by the shear excitement of becoming successful and the lure of making lots of money. I love earning income and being paid for helping others. I also freely admit: I'm a bona fide, card-carrying serial entrepreneur.

As I shared with you earlier, for most of my life, I considered myself an entrepreneur who played a television news anchor on TV! I spent twenty-five years delivering the news in cities like my hometown of Detroit, Michigan; Dayton, Ohio; and Pittsburgh, Pennsylvania. I was always aware I could take the same lessons I had learned and applied in the television news industry and use them to launch and sustain any business. I learned a lot about how to gain the trust of others and how to manage competition.

Perhaps the biggest lessons I have learned, I've never forgotten, and I use them every day in business. They are:

- Give great value.
- Be consistently good at what you do.
- Provide an exceptional product or service.
- Find more ways for people to know, like, and trust you.
- Display a clear message that you are dependable and reliable.
- Face the competition and beat them.

At the television stations that I worked at, those are the things we strived for, news hour after news hour. The fight to become the number-one-watched news station in the market is challenging, yet rewarding. It taught me a lot, and I leveraged that drive in my own personal life and business. I always had a deeper calling. My desire was to challenge myself in ways only entrepreneurs are familiar with, not necessarily news anchors. I yearned to expose that desire and I looked for opportunities to start my own business.

After all, I had already figured it all out at the age of eight with Bam Bam's Juicy Juice Stand! (I'm only partially joking!) That is where I remember building my foundation for entrepreneurial success. My experience afforded me the opportunity to know what it was like to create something in my mind and actually see it come to fruition. Best of all, I had no fear. As a child I was unapologetically being me and didn't understand the emotions of fear and doubt that often hold so many adults back.

I had the pride of making this special orange juice concoction, sharing it with others, and then celebrating when I earned money from it. I call this "The Entrepreneur's Trifecta!"

Now granted, we are talking about a twenty-five-cent orange juice stand. But it was a big time operation in my mind at the age of eight. I remember I got the neighborhood kids involved. We held team meetings. We decorated old cardboard boxes with crayons and even did some door to door marketing.

I had the front end of operations running, but the back end…well, that presented a challenge. Oranges were expensive back then, plus they didn't yield much, and when I needed help from the kids to squeeze them, my team had vanished.

I was also practicing the four things that I practice consistently today. I now call them my "Four Pillars for Success": leadership, leverage, lifestyle, and loving your journey.

Although I'd consequently figured out the concepts of leadership and leverage at eight years old, I hadn't figured out the lifestyle and loving the journey parts. I was miserable. I spent several days with sore hands, locked up inside the house squeezing oranges on those summer afternoons. The oranges that seemed so sweet somehow soured in my hands. The taste of success wasn't so pleasant, and this project of mine all of a sudden felt so strained.

But I couldn't give up. I had set out toward a goal, and I was not going to stop until I saw my glass jar filled up with quarters and I saw a few satisfied customers enjoying my Bam Bam's Juicy Juice. So I squeezed as many oranges as my poor little hands could squeeze until they just couldn't squeeze another drop, and I begged my grandmother for her assistance. She helped me load my Juicy Juice with lots of sugar, water, and red Kool-Aid packages to fancy it up. I dragged my colorful stand, my tasty product, and my bruised pride out to the end of her driveway.

Now, not to be completely undone by the other neighborhood kids who had copied me and constructed similar operations, I did make a few sales. In fact, I even turned a profit, though not much. The value for me back then was not so much the chump change or what I considered hard work. It was what I learned, the valuable lessons of finishing what you start, being proud of what you create, and working toward achieving your dream, no matter what obstacles arise.

I dare you to dream bigger! I dare you to take the mask off, the disguise you've been wearing that's stopping you from complete authenticity. I invite you to declare, right now, what you want to be, do, and have.

I want you to get clear on what's holding you back. I want you to bravely look at your mistakes—because we've all made mistakes—and embrace those you refuse to take responsibility for. Be okay with the journey you have been on thus far, that has led you here to this transforming place in time. Get completely naked in front of the mirror of your "now" and bare all, mistakes included. Without those mistakes, you miss learning the valuable lessons that are allowing you to readjust your course and gain clarity. Mistakes are not roadblocks but blessings in disguise.

THE BUTTERFLY ANALOGY

An entrepreneur is similar to a caterpillar in some ways. When the world sees him, he is just another creepy crawler with potential. What's within him dictates his future. Even though it is not apparent to the human eye what he is to become, he has a secret that will be revealed at an appointed time. His main focus now is survival. If he can exist in his habitat, awaiting that special moment when his secret is to be discovered, then he will become something beautiful.

He awakens one morning, expecting to go about his daily routine, and something inside him shouts, "Today is the day!" He stops eating, and to all the other creepy crawlers in the animal kingdom, it appears as if he's going to die. Instead, he crawls up a low-hanging tree, finds a twig, and spins himself a silky cocoon, a shiny chrysalis that is only a hint of what's to come. Within his protective casing, the caterpillar endures a major change, shedding the old and transforming into something new. When his metamorphosis is complete, he emerges as a beautiful butterfly, taking flight and ready to fulfill his God-given destiny.

I encourage you to shed off everything that will not transform you, change you, or move you toward the direction you choose to go. Those who cannot relinquish old habits and restrictive beliefs are prohibited from moving forward into their destiny. You have to be willing to change. It's okay to let go of the collateral damage you've been collecting and storing in your mind and heart. It will not diminish who you are but propel you onto the backstage of your destiny.

If you are truly ready, it's show time!

SHOWTIME

It's time to get onto the stage of life, pull back the curtain, and show the world what you are made of. If you have been hiding and playing small, you are giving your power away, power you need to create the kind of life you may be dreaming of. We've all been blessed with the innate ability to dream big. We often let fears and doubts get in the way of accomplishing whatever we are dreaming about. We each possess unique talents and gifts that, when tapped into, become the source for making our dreams come true.

There are so many ways to express what you are good at. Often you can become an expert in a field or area or industry waiting for a newcomer like you. You could be just the right person with a fresh approach that others are looking for. You might be the neophyte who has a unique idea or different way of doing things that changes the way an entire industry functions. It's time to stop hiding and play all out! Go for it! Unleash your passions and see what you can create!

The world needs that special thing that you have.

THAT SPECIAL THING

It's about bettering the lives of others, being a part of something bigger than just you, and making a positive difference. You don't have to be Mother Teresa, Gandhi, or the next bestselling author. Really impacting other people's lives is about choosing to be more and to have more purpose around what you're passionate about.

Helen Keller lost her hearing and sight as a toddler after becoming ill. This is one of the most unimaginable misfortunes for a young child and their family. But as we know, she became a world-renowned author, speaker, and social activist despite her disabilities.

You're reading this, so I clearly know you can see, so what's stopping you from walking in your exceptionality? Seriously, what has you bound to mediocrity?

We often use any excuse to stop us, many of them lame and ridiculous. We forget just how fortunate we really are, and yet we are quick to worry and complain and be held back by the smallest things. It is said that Helen Keller not only accomplished those great things even with her handicap, but she was focused on "a worthy purpose." In other words she made her mission all about serving others, and her purpose drove her. She turned her passion into a means of helping others, in spite of all of her personal limitations.

I want you to know just how blessed you really are. You likely face lesser challenges than Helen Keller, and look at what she achieved with her passion to make a difference in the world!

Life is about more than having a lot of stuff; it is also about being many things, and having the opportunity to experience different facets of who you are by striving to enjoy a host of diverse opportunities that await your attention.

As I'm sure you already know, you can be rich beyond measure and still be miserable. I know many people with perfect bodies who still aren't happy with the way that they look. I also know people who have plenty of time on their hands but simply do nothing with it, as well as those who complain about not having enough stuff though they live cluttered lives with many toys and trinkets. Taking your mask off and living your truth means fully experiencing all that you have, all that you're becoming, and all that you're doing. You must embrace life and then find ways to give and serve others in the process.

Jim Morrison, the lead singer for *The Doors*, had this to say about masks:

> "The most important kind of freedom is to be what you really are. You trade in your reality for a role. You trade in your sense for an act. You give up your ability to feel, and in exchange, put on a mask. There can't be any large-scale revolution until there's a personal revolution, on an individual level. It's got to happen inside first."

When we declare that we will take our masks off and be true to our passions, we must be dedicated to our self-mastery. We must be determined and disciplined about what motivates us, stay true to our sense of self, and remain on our own path.

Sometimes it's hard to decide to break free from conformity and drive our own pursuits towards fulfilling our dreams. Often this may result in an intense personal struggle as you attempt to extend yourself beyond your current place of being. Even more so, as you fully dedicate yourself to living your passions, it may annoy some people around you. It could injure some egos, step on some toes, split a few relationships, and force wedges in places we previously found to be safe ground.

Pulling back the mask and being who you are is hard work. First, it will require you to face your internal doubts. Then, it will dictate that you find new practices of joy and a greater sense of gratitude. But it can be done—it must be done if you are to unleash your passions and share them with the world.

"I AM" STATEMENTS

I am a firm believer in creating "I Am" statements. These are bold and affirmative action declarations. These statements proclaim and pronounce in the present who you are. I believe creating and announcing "I Am" statements gets you into the creation process faster and really ramps up universal flow.

The universe is awaiting your instruction, be it negative or positive. Stating a declaration such as "I Am a success" will render an optimistic reply from the universe. Positive affirmations will bring positive change in your life.

Make "I Am" statements like:

- I am a strong and confident business owner.
- I am bold and courageous.
- I am attracting all the right people, resources, opportunities, and accomplishments right now to lead to my success.
- I am successful.
- I am wealthy.
- I am earning exponentially more and more each and every month!

You can go on and on with this and get really empowered. I realize for some people this is tough and it takes time. I coach a whole series on "I Am" statements, where I help people boldly step out of fear and what is holding them back, and step into the "now" of creating what they really want, living the life they have always dreamed about.

I encourage you to create and start declaring your "I Am" statements. Print them out and place them on your bathroom mirror, refrigerator door, near your computer, on the dashboard of your car, or on your nightstand next to your bed. Place your "I Am" statements where you can see them on a daily basis. Now you will be reminded constantly of who you are, who you are becoming, and just how amazing life can be.

When you are running a business, there are so many things to think about: employees, receipts, customer tracking, orders, bills, payroll, contracts…I could go on and on, right?

Sometimes we lose focus on why we started the journey in the first place. Let me remind you to quiet the noise and sink a little deeper into your "I Am" proclamations. This can help you find balance in the unavoidable daily chaos of running your business and help you avoid being frazzled and burned out. Trust me, I know. Burn-out can happen faster than you think. It can feel like a rush of heaviness and emotions, darkening your judgment and making your vision cloudy. When this happens to me—because I'm so busy juggling so much—I find some quiet time to attract the balance and peace I need to enjoy a successful business and lifestyle. I pray, meditate, run, and do an activity that helps me focus on something other than the issue that's stressing me. I go back to my "I Am" statements and repeat them out loud so I can gain clarity and strength.

Make it a point to create some powerful "I Am" statements and repeat them often. Be sure to remind yourself of your own greatness by proclaiming them in the present tense. See them happening now; declare them, in spite of the opposite happenings that might be showing up. This process can open you up to wonderful, synchronistic opportunities that seem to magically appear, all because you firmly declare who you are!

ACTION PLAN

Explore how the world sees you when you take off your mask and become your authentic self. Take some quiet time and answer these questions. Then ask someone who knows you best to answer these questions about you. Compare your answers.

QUESTIONS

1. Are you hiding, playing small, and not unleashing your passion for whatever reasons?
2. Are you giving of yourself?
3. How many ways can you think of to support others?

HUSTLE TIP

"I just don't have an addiction to the outcome."

- Ray Higdon, Founder at Team Start Living and Author, Speaker, and Network Marketer - *Hustle & Heart TV* on Episode 9

HEART TIP:

"How am I inspiring my kids to the life that they are going to grow into?"

- Ray Higdon, Founder at Team Start Living and Author, Speaker, and Network Marketer - *Hustle & Heart TV* on Episode 9

CHAPTER FOUR
A POWERFUL SENSE OF PURPOSE

Knowing Your "Why" and Your Goals

There comes a time in the lives of those destined for greatness when we must stand before the mirror of meaning and ask, "Why, having been endowed with the courageous heart of a lion, do we live as mice?"

-Brendon Burchard-

If you are finding it difficult to set goals, take a moment to think about *why* you want what you want. When you are genuinely 100 percent committed to reaching your goals, you move from hoping that you will achieve them to knowing you will. If we want something badly enough, then quitting is simply not an option.

Successful individuals, who strive to reach their goals with an intense, burning need to achieve them, are often referred to as being "driven." This special quality is not reserved only for a privileged few. You can have it, too.

With the right approach, anyone can cultivate a deep, passionate want within themselves and move to a state of total commitment to that objective. You can know with certainty that success is as inevitable as the sun rising each morning and setting each night.

Think about this: What if you could do more than just get things done, complete the tasks, and add another checkmark to your to-do list? What if you could reach beyond competence and mediocrity and strive for excellence?

I believe the secret to doing great things and becoming habitual about unleashing your passion is recognizing a few things about yourself and having a "why." Equally important is remembering that your potential is pretty much limitless, a point backed up by science. Years of research and observation suggest that we only fully understand about 5 percent of how our minds and bodies work, and therefore only *use* 5 percent. We have so much more to give.

You'll do three things when you understand the value of discovering your "why":

1. You will better understand your own motivation and willingness to succeed.
2. You will be able to better motivate yourself when you know your deepest reasons for wanting something, and you can be driven from that point.
3. You will be able to identify whether you have the solutions in front of you or you need to go out and find them or even create them.

If you don't know your "why" and you haven't yet identified your goals, it's going to be tough to work toward reaching them.

You need to have a "why." You need to have a "why" that is so deep and emotional for you that living without it is not an option. Your "why" needs to make you cry. It also needs to fuel you and keep you fighting for what you want.

You must have a crystal clear goal that you continuously see before you that inspires you to accomplish it, no matter what it takes to make it a reality.

Do you know what your goals are? Do you know why you want them? Having the goal and knowing your "why" is how you get started, but nothing will happen until you take action.

Your passion fuels your actions.

Ask yourself: what am I willing to do, become, learn, or experience to unleash my passion in the direction of my goals?

I can assure you that my success has everything to do with dreaming big, working hard and hustling. When I started *Hustle & Heart TV*—my video podcast show, my latest entrepreneurial pursuit—I knew that I needed to unleash a new "why." I knew up until then that I had either achieved some of my other goals, or I was aimlessly striking at things that weren't adding up. Besides, for this venture, I would need to spend countless hours learning how to podcast, learning new equipment and marketing approaches, and brand new ways of doing business. I had to focus deeply on *why* I was going to spend all of this time and money to launch a new business.

I've invested thousands of dollars with successful coaches, trainers, and mentors. I've also had the great fortune to interview several top notch entrepreneurs, industry leaders, authors and trainers, celebrities, educators, community activists, and top-earning network marketers and Internet gurus. Throughout my years of reading, watching, and listening to successful and inspiring people, I've learned quite a bit.

A strong "why" is the one thing passion-inspired and successful entrepreneurs all have. They have a clear and definite purpose and intention with a clear and definitive outcome. Their "why" is the catalyst for what they are doing and what they are creating and what they are giving service and life and light to. It is this "why" that drives them. It is their passion, and they unleash it every chance they get, every single day in the direction of achieving their goals. It's a vision that is crystal clear. Their "why" has great meaning, and it serves as their tangible truth.

Let me ask you again: do you have a very clear "why" that drives you, that fuels you, that provides the fire in your belly to get up and go after what it is you want?

Congratulations if you have it. Keep hustling for it and stay focused on it and never give up. If you don't have a "why," and you're still searching for it, it's okay. When you become more intimate with pursuing your passion and you set some goals, your "why" will naturally emerge. Sometimes our "why" comes to us when we least expect it. For others, their "why" is staring them right in their face, but they're looking past it because they haven't connected with it.

Our "why's" can change and often do. But when we have them and we are certain we can't live without them, we are like an exhausted marathon runner, steps away from the finish line, unstoppable and relentless about crossing it.

I challenge you to find your "why" or to focus more deeply on it, or to find a new one if your old "why" is worn-out or out-of-date. It will serve as the driving force when you ask these two questions: "Why am I giving up?" or "Why am I doing this?" As you can tell, establishing your "why" is a key component in your hustle.

GOALS

The next key trait many successful people share is having clear goals. Let's take a look at some of the more commonly expressed goals:

- Lose weight
- Great relationships
- Get rich
- Buy a new car
- Quit my job
- Retire early
- Get out of debt
- Get a new house
- Take a vacation
- Work from home
- Fund my children's education
- Spend more time with family
- Spend more time doing the things I love
- Be more philanthropic
- Travel more
- Have the ability to make a difference
- Help others achieve their goals
- Time freedom

- Financial freedom
- Funding a new venture

Some of these may be on your goals list, too. They all are exciting and rewarding goals to have.

Now, let's look at the "why" behind some of these goals. Your "why" is the deep-rooted emotion around having and achieving your goals, thus it is tied closely to your goals. When your "why" is intrinsic and priceless and it touches your very depths, the goal means more. You will fight, scratch, and work hard, long hours to reach that goal because your "why" is driving you. Make your "why" so big it excites you, pushes you, empowers you, and leaves you wanting more.

Having a powerful "why" is an adrenaline infusion that provides the strength and endurance to overcome the unavoidable trials, troubles, and challenges that go with striving for any goal. Sensible and safe "whys" leave us restricted to mediocrity, only allowing us to use a moderate amount of ambition. We are left uninspired. Average ambition only leaves us with enough fuel to get through the first or second set of problems we face on the way to reaching our goals, at which point we can easily throw in the towel and give up, blaming it on the circumstance at the moment. If the "why" is mediocre or average, the effort will be ordinary and so will the results. In other words, don't play it safe—dream big and bold, and support those dreams with a fantastic "why."

I believe when you set a goal fueled by a strong "why," it should energize you, excite you, and give your passion full of meaning and purpose. It should exhilarate you and give you the assurance that you're headed in the right direction.

If we can stay focused on the outcome and centered on what it is that we want and the "why" of wanting it, we are guaranteed to stay on the right road. In addition, if we face the obstacles that will come up along the way, and we don't allow ourselves to get in our own way, then we can surely reach our intended destination.

GO BIG

Dream big, take no prisoners, and think way outside of the box. Go explore what it would mean to have the things you are dreaming about. Schedule some house tours. Watch videos about the places you want to travel to. Talk with people who are doing the things you want to do. Start finding things to cement your dreams in your future reality, and don't make the common mistake of thinking and rationalizing yourself out of having your dream. It's very easy to do.

Let's say you want a brand new shiny white Range Rover loaded and packed with all the extras. You can see yourself driving around the neighborhood and up and down the streets in this big, beautiful SUV. You go out to take a test drive. You hop in, take a whiff of the new car smell, run your hands across the smooth leather interior, turn up the music, and hit the ignition. It's the ride of your life! It feels good, and you look good in it. You take home one of those fancy brochures. You even put it up someplace in the house where you can look at it every day. You start to think, 'Yes…this is my baby!'

Boom, it happens. Doubt steps in, and because your goal is not anchored by a strong "why," you start to think, "Wait a minute, I can't afford this. There's no way I can come up with that kind of money!" You start looking at your current bills, income, and overall financial position, and justify not being able to have it.

Next, another set of challenges swoop in. Perhaps a larger than expected electric bill comes due or the kids need some extra football equipment. Perhaps the contact that you thought was going to land you that great account falls through, or your air conditioning unit in your home goes out. Whatever the reason, you stop looking at the photos of the Range Rover, and you stop dreaming. You begin to settle. Then, to make yourself feel better, you even start to talk yourself out of your dream. You start to say things like, "Wow, what was I thinking in the first place? I can't afford that! Besides, what would other people say about me?" Deep, ugly thoughts start to fill your head and you think, 'I'm not worthy of this. I don't deserve that SUV, anyway.'

The self-doubt begins to set in. You slowly slip away from believing in yourself and your ability to achieve your goals. You put yourself in your own way. You let the obstacles facing you—the unexpected bills, the failed relationships, the clients that don't show up and buy your product or services—begin to define your result.

I've done it. I see it happening every single day. I'm using an SUV as an example, but think of the countless times we settled for not achieving our goal when the obstacles arose. We settled for the common and lost sight of our "why." When we reengineer our objective to be focused on the "why" behind the goal, we are more likely to advance bravely toward it. We must be "uncommon" with why we want our goals.

UNCOMMON

Having that shiny new 80k Range Rover is like living an uncommon lifestyle. None of us are common or just average, and you deserve the best if that's what you want.

We sometimes force ourselves into a common existence by limiting our mindset about what's possible. If you truly want to achieve happiness through achieving your goals and dreams, then you have to get into a different mindset. Know that in order to have an uncommon lifestyle, you will need to develop the uncommon habit of making uncommon decisions. When times get tough and obstacles arise, you can face them with an uncommon approach.

Decide and declare that having your new SUV—or whatever your goal—is of chief importance to you. Imagine yourself with the reward you are dreaming about. Get intimate with having your goals. Feel yourself in possession of what you desire. Visualize yourself owning your dream. How would that make you feel?

Own your goal and your "why." It's yours. See it, claim it, embrace it, and simply expect it. Be clear about having it. Have laser focus that keeps you dead on target, and anticipate the obstacles that are sure to try to get in your way. Expect them and vow to hit the mark anyhow. This will help to keep you centered when the doubts and unexpected events happen in life. Get focused and stay focused!

FOCUS

Simply put, you get what you focus on. Where your focus goes, your energy flows. When your energy flows, whatever you are focusing on will grow. In other words, your life is controlled by what you focus on. That's why you need to focus on where you want to go, what you want to see happening, how you want to feel, and what you want to become or gain.

Do not focus on what you fear, hate, loathe, or are uncertain about. Do not focus on problems. Instead, focus on solutions. The next time you find yourself in a state of uncertainty, resist your fear; shift your focus deliberately toward where you want to go, and your actions will take you in that direction.

ACTION PLAN

Get clear on your goals, and be intentional. State your "why."

Create an action plan that is broken down in daily, weekly, and monthly goals. Write them down, and post them so you can see them daily.

Find pictures, words or images that you can paste on a dream board and put it where you can see it daily!

QUESTIONS

Here are some questions to ask yourself:

1. What is your "why"?

2. What's your deadline? When do you want this?

3. Who do you need to contact today to help you move closer to getting your "why"?

4. What three things have you been avoiding that you can do today to get closer to figuring out your "why" and achieving your goals?

5. What would you do if there were no way you could fail?

6. If you were ten times smarter than the rest of the world, what would your goal be?

7. If there were no obstacles in your way, what would you dream of doing?

HUSTLE TIP

"Learn to be a hunter. Every single day, go out and learn what you need to accomplish that day, that will get you closer to your goal."

- Nicole Cooper, Internet Marketer and Speaker -
Hustle & Heart TV on Episode 16

HEART TIP

"Identify what you love to do and the things that you find yourself being drawn close to, and figure out how you can build a business model around it."

- Nicole Cooper, Internet Marketer and Speaker -
Hustle & Heart TV on Episode 16

CHAPTER FIVE

FEARLESS AND BRAVE

Push Past the Things Holding You Back

I learned that courage was not the absence of fear
but the triumph over it. The brave man is not he who
does not feel afraid but he who conquers that fear.

-Nelson Mandela-

B y now you have come to realize that our thoughts more so than our circumstances sabotage our freedom and success. We are the ones who allow our insecurities and fears to grow into a tidal wave of worry that washes away our dreams. We are the ones who constantly delay our own progress, stalling out just when we need courage to carry on.

What are you putting off doing, becoming, or having out of fear of succeeding?

What you fear doing is what you most need to do.

Fear is the most prominent force that holds us back from doing more, from being more, and from having more. It's the fear that we might fail in what we want to become, what we want to do, or in getting what we want to have that trips us up on the road to success.

What's even more tragic is the fact that we never get started because of these false beliefs of self-doubt and fear of failure.

Ultimately, it is fear of the unknown that prevents us from doing what we need to do.

What are you afraid of? If you are afraid of something, it is stopping you from moving forward and paralyzing you in your tracks. Fear shuts down the circuitry in your brain. It is a biological response that will actually force you to freeze up. If you feel stuck right now in your life, it is likely because a fear of something is keeping you there.

Instead of overcoming fear, too many people defend it. You think to yourself, 'But what if it doesn't work? What if I can't do it? What if something happens?' Then you settle for less, because you are afraid of the "What if's?"

Fear is meant to be a defense mechanism that tells your brain that you are in imminent danger. Usually, fear is a lie.

Fear should not control how you live your life or make your decisions. It really is all in your mind. As a man thinks, so he is. What you think, you speak. What you speak, you believe. What you believe, you will receive.

There can be no real progress if we endlessly question our own course of action and our capabilities based on the fear of the unknown. The greatest damage from fear isn't what we fail in doing—it is who we fail to become.

It is okay to be afraid; we all have past experiences of failure, mistakes, and hurt. However, it is not okay to let fear control you or keep you where you are! The truth is what you feed will flourish, and what you neglect will die. Your fears will grow or shrink, depending on what you choose to focus on. You must choose to starve your fear and feed your faith. You were not designed to live in fear, worry, or anxiety. You were designed to live a faith-filled life, an adventurous life, a life of freedom.

Fear affects your decision-making, your confidence, and your ability to reach your goals. Fear will keep you from taking risks. You might be limiting yourself right now without even realizing it!

A bold, solid decision and swift action can kill fear.

Don't be afraid like the rest of the world. 80 percent of people are convinced they are incapable of achieving great things. Therefore, they safely aim for mediocrity. Ironically, the level of competition is fiercest when one is trying to reach sensible goals.

We could all choose to be limited by our fears and doubts. I'm not suggesting that some fears are not real. We face many different types of limiting situations: scarce resources, finite possibilities, boundaries, barriers, challenges, and deadlines. These are stark realities not to be confused with things we should be fearful about. Fear is something different. It can rip us from our greatness and destroy our potential. Fear and doubt are like demonic archangels, steering us away from our God-entrusted desires. When we allow fear to be a constant in our lives, our ambitions and behaviors become small and constrained. We withdraw. We become stressed and timid. We lose our center and focus.

It is time that we push past fear and doubt, and decide to manage its foul control in our hearts and minds. We must learn to embrace and engage the emotions we are having and not allow fear to control our decision-making. Fear and doubt are a natural course of change. They will always be present, especially when we are thinking of doing something new and different. When we admit that we have allowed fear and doubt to hold us back from our passions, then we can use them to propel us forward instead.

Expecting the worst is one of the greatest controls that fear has over us. We're scared to do something because we think it will be too hard on us. We think we're not capable, ready, worthy, and we allow these doubts to stop us. If we could only remember that these are common emotions that everyone undergoes. Most great accomplishments were achieved by people who were afraid at first. People who, with no idea about what they were doing or what the result would be, pushed past their fear to bring their dream to life. We can break through these thought patterns when we take a moment to realize that we have learned and endured more difficult life experiences despite of fear. Once again we can learn and embrace new experiences *now*. Maybe we can even imagine ourselves enjoying what fear can teach us about ourselves versus struggling with it. Imagine the worst case scenario, then imagine the best. Acknowledge that the reality will be somewhere in between the two, and work to make it closer to the best case scenario.

Use fear and failure as your tutor and your teacher. Don't let these forces navigate you away from what you are intended to become. You are resilient, you are strong, you are unapologetic, and you are more than capable and much stronger than your fears and doubts. What you have to share with the world is necessary, and your gifts, talents, and passions deserve the exposure that only you can bring to them. Let your light shine and let fear dim to just a shadow.

You are also armed with your "why," your greatest weapon against fear.

When you are facing something challenging, when you are doubting your direction, when you fear making a decision, I invite you to use my personal mantra.

Find a mirror, stand in front of it and repeat after me:

"I will not be made less by my fears, doubts and challenges. Instead, I will be made more by the promise of God and this universe that abundance, joy, prosperity, and peace are mine now and forever more."

ACTION PLAN

Instead of spreading fear today, how about you spread a message of unbelievable faith and courage? Today, I want you to ask yourself, "What am I afraid of?" What would you do with your life if you knew you would not fail? If there was a 100 percent chance of success, would you take it?

What is it costing you financially, emotionally, and physically to postpone action because of fear? Is it worth it to not go after your dream?

It is equally important to measure the odious cost of inaction. If you don't chase those things that excite you, where will you be in one, five, or ten years from now?

How will you feel having allowed circumstances to impose themselves on you? How will you feel having allowed ten more years of your finite life to pass by doing what you already know does not fulfill you?

What are you waiting for?

HUSTLE TIP

"Never stop hustling. What I see in this industry is we get clients and we have a good month, and then the next month we sort of sit back and relax... there is no relaxing this. Business is fast-growing, and someone is always there to step up into where you are. It never stops; it's always a hustle, hustle, hustle, getting out there, high visibility. That means webinars, that means podcasts that means video challenges, teleseminars, being out there, being seen, live events. Hustle all the time to stay in the forefront of your desired ideal audience."

- Stephanie Donegan, Coach and Client Magnet Specialist - *Hustle & Heart TV* on Episode 6

HEART TIP

"Love what you do. Create the business around what you really love to do. Discover what it is you love and then intertwine that to your business, and every day will be a day that you wake up full of gratitude for the life that you live."

- Stephanie Donegan, Coach and Client Magnet Specialist - *Hustle & Heart TV* on Episode 6

CHAPTER SIX

LOVE AND SELF-ACCEPTANCE

Balance and Purpose

If you celebrate your differentness, the world will, too.
It believes exactly what you tell it—through the words you
use to describe yourself, the actions you take to care for yourself,
and the choices you make to express yourself. Tell the world you
are a one-of-a-kind creation who came here to experience
wonder and spread joy. Expect to be accommodated.

-Victoria Moran-

Back in 2000 I did something that even baffled the minds of those who were in my inner circle. I quit my job as a news anchor at WPXI Channel 11 News in Pittsburgh to work from home with a network marketing company. I was driven by the desire to be at home with my son, who was in kindergarten. I couldn't fathom the idea of sending him away to school in the morning and not seeing him until the next morning because I was working from 3pm to midnight. That sacrifice was too big to make. So I quit, with my son as my "why." I went full force into creating a successful network marketing team with Market America.

I spent four years at home with him until WPXI made me a great offer to return to the evening news set. I decided to head back to the anchor desk.

I missed my friends and colleagues and the busy pace of delivering breaking news. It felt good to be back in the saddle—the anchor chair—and I looked forward to being a trusted voice and face on Pittsburgh TV once again.

But it wasn't meant to last forever. I felt myself staving off the desire to go back into business. I hid in the proverbial closet and did not actively seek an entrepreneurial opportunity for about eight years. That decade came and went with the same kind of boring day in and day out, mundane routine of going to work: the same activities, no real challenges, no real need to explore or dig a little deeper, no real excitement, no real chance to create and explore. I was denying myself the privilege of living the entrepreneurial lifestyle, something that I was destined to do all my life.

I can look back now and know I was hiding from my desire and passion to be in business for myself and impact the lives of others in a significant way.

I began to turn that energy toward a physical expression. I started running marathons, working out daily, and getting into shape, and by 2010 I had even started pole dancing! (Now before your mind goes someplace it shouldn't, pole dancing is an awesome workout. You get into amazing shape, and women and men have so much fun doing it.) My problem was where could a television news anchor discretely go to take pole dancing lessons? Seriously, you can imagine a major news operation would not take too kindly to its top news anchor pole dancing! I was hooked!

I started lessons and began enjoying how physically strong I had become. I had so much pride in this taboo form of exercise and was constantly wishing pole dancing wasn't so negatively looked upon. "It's exercise, for God's sake," I can remember telling my friends. "It's the fastest way I know how to build muscle and have fun." Still, I worried about my reputation and what the public would think. I wished there was a studio that was just like a regular fitness club that I could walk into and learn to pole dance without the stigma and stares. People go into gyms and fitness studios every day and pick up a weight and pump iron without funny looks and criticism!

Then it happened. I was sitting at my kitchen table and the thought hit me: *Open your own studio*! Create a fun, safe, respectable place where professional women could learn to pole dance without feeling ashamed or embarrassed.

I was so engrossed with the idea that I envisioned opening a studio that would allow people to try a myriad of other different workouts as well. This fitness studio would incorporate programs for aerial yoga, aerial silk dance, ballet barre, trapeze, lyra, hip hop dance, and of course, pole dance.

Fullbody Fitness Club was born. I could write several chapters on how this incredible and exciting fitness playground in the South Hills of Pittsburgh came to be. What happened in three years was of divine inspiration, born of passion and desire. It was amazing how the pieces all seemed to fall into place, with the best instructors, support, and members a woman could ever ask for. It had to be God and the universe saying "Yes" to my asking and my belief.

Some might have called it a miracle. I didn't know the first thing about opening a fitness studio. I didn't even have the instructors and aerialists in my database. By the way, try looking up "aerialist" in the Yellow Pages. They don't exist.

What did exist was my heartfelt desire, my passion and commitment to creating a space where people could transform their work out and awaken their spirit; a fun fitness environment where people could try new things; a place where people had the freedom to be who they are, with no judgment and no criticism.

The more I told the story, the more I believed it and saw this great vision unfolding, the more excited and talented instructors came pouring into my life. It was as if God and the universe uniquely crafted this, and it was through me this beautiful fitness playground was born into the world. I don't doubt this is precisely how Fullbody came to be.

In the beginning things were running along smoothly, and then BOOM: financial trouble started lurking on the horizon! Eight months in, I needed a way to pay the light bill. There were lots of overhead expenses, and sixteen instructors and two people coming to classes was a formula for disaster. The entrepreneur startup honeymoon was over. It was time to get down to business.

In May 2012, I began a distributorship with It Works! Global and began selling those "Crazy Wraps", The Ultimate Body Applicators. This amazing product helps you tone, tighten, and firm in forty- five minutes for only $25. I thought, 'Bingo! Everybody wants an easy, quick fix to looking better.' So I plowed headfirst into creating another stream of income to help with the expenses at the studio.

I have been involved in several network marketing, or MLM—Multi-Level Marketing—companies in the past, and I know the work and dedication it takes. To be a success, you have to build a team and pour your energy and passion into helping them become successful. That's the beauty of network marketing; you don't have to do it all by yourself. But what I wasn't prepared for was how quickly this new venture would take off and just how many people needed this business vehicle as a means of making money and starting their own home-based businesses. The money started rolling in, and the studio also started doing well.

I started dreaming again. If I could get my income from It Works! Global to a point where I could afford to quit my job at WPXI again, that would be awesome. The time had come for me to seriously consider this. I had a new passion and a new "why," but could I do it?

Admittedly, I was exhausted. I was so busy working at the TV station, running the fitness studio, selling those "Crazy Wraps", and building my It Works team, I had no time for my life, my husband Arnold, and, most importantly, our son, who was months away from heading into his senior year of high school. I had already missed out on so much of Tre's life working the night shift at the television station. I was missing the things that were most important to him—his Friday night football games. I can't tell you how this pained me. I felt guilty and desperate. The sacrifices we make for our children are infinite, and I couldn't afford to miss out on our precious time together. I had to make a huge shift and it needed to come quickly.

I set a goal to make enough money with It Works! Global to match my six-figure income at WPXI, so I could quit my job. I was determined this had to happen.

January of 2013, I got off an airplane from an annual It Works! Global conference in Florida. Tre was there to pick me up. I was ready—I had been rolling this pressing thought around in my head and heart for a couple of months, and now was the time to get serious about it.

When I got in the car, I looked at Tre and said, "Buddy…" (I know. I can't believe I was still calling a seventeen-year-old "Buddy"!) Anyway, I said, "Buddy, I'm quitting my job as a TV news anchor by September so I can spend as much time with you in your senior year and finally make it to your football games!"

Tre looked back into my eyes…and said, "Mom would you do that for me?"

I'll never forget those words and how they plunged deep inside me. I pulled back for air, with tears welling up in my eyes and my stomach full of guilt and emotion from having not spent enough time with him in the first place. I stared back and said, "Tre, of course I would. You're my baby, and I love you."

BOOM, a new dream, a new "why," and a new passion was born.

I had to work fast to get things done. I had just confessed to the very person that I love the most in the world that I was going to make this huge shift in our lives…and there was no letting him down.

There was now even more pressure to deal with. I had less than nine months to get the money to do it, and with even less time on my hands. I had to hustle.

So I went to work. I started busting my butt selling those "Crazy Wraps", I was working three and four parties a weekend, holding trainings and meetings, and working to build my distributor team. I had set a big goal because I had a big "why." I was determined to become a top money earner with It Works! Global and be able to walk away from a stable six-figure salary.

I did it! In four months of setting that goal back in January 2013, I not only matched my income, I surpassed it and ended that year as the 54th highest paid distributor in a company with over 70,000 distributors.

Needless to say, I retired from WPXI in September of 2013 and ended up attending all but one of Tre's high school football games. (By the way, his team, Pittsburgh Central Catholic, dominated that year, going all the way to the state finals and ending his 2013 as the WPIAL AAAA Champions and runner-up in the PIAA AAAA State Championship.) My son is now attending college at Vanderbilt University in Tennessee, and I have the time and financial freedom to travel to see his football games and cheer him on from the stands.

Here's what I know about successful people in business: They are proud of their multiple attempts at trying and failing. No matter what, they love and accept themselves. They are okay with being out of balance for a short time when they are busy working on a project. But they also know how important it is to find balance and enjoy the journey. They determined long ago that it doesn't matter how many times they try, how many dreams they have, or how many hits and misses are adding up on their scoreboard in life. Successful entrepreneurs have keen ideas and passions. They learn to promote or produce products and services that support those passions, and they do it with great pride and purpose.

LOVE YOUR JOURNEY

None of your success is worth it if you do not love the process of getting there. It is imperative to love your journey!

Success is defined in many different ways. Most people, arguably, would define success as achieving a goal. 99 percent of your time is spent aggressively trying to realize and accomplish your goal. Why not also see success happening in every second and every moment you are working toward achieving the end result?

Let's start celebrating those little things you are doing that will make you successful in life, the things that will secure your health, your happiness, your dreams, and your fulfillment. Those simple, tiny, unnoticeable routines that you will do day in and day out are the building blocks of working consistently toward your goal. Besides, if you are not enjoying the small steps along your journey, you will likely not do them, and you will eventually fail in reaching your goal.

In fact, this is why only five out of a hundred people working toward any goal ever really achieve it. The other 95 give up. It gets too hard. They don't enjoy the hard work and dedication. It takes consistent action, no matter what, despite all circumstances and obstacles, to remain focused while bearing toward your results.

The choices you make today, compounded by patience and time, with a sincere effort and a strong knowing and belief, is how you sail closer toward living and realizing your dream. You have to remain active. You have to remain consistent. You have to remain focused and prepared. You are attracting and preparing to receive what it is that you have been asking for.

Don't be like those who give up way too soon because the hard work and the hustle were more than they were willing to do. Don't let the no's, the naysayers, the doubters, or the disbelief of others sway you from finding and living your passion. This is what takes out so many people who say they want success, but aren't willing to ignore their critics. You can break free from the negative influences that surround you, from the nonsupportive people in your life and from the downward pull of life circumstances and challenges that you face in life. But first you must choose to accept, on some level, that you are attracting this. You are vibrating this negative energy, and it's showing up as obstacles and naysayers in your life. You can break this by changing your focus, taking responsibility, and loving yourself just as you are.

My son will tell you, because I've drilled into his head, "You get what you focus on. Period." When he was little and just starting out with football, he would get so upset after losing a game. He would complain and grumble about how badly they lost and how he and his team were no good and would never win. He would go on for hours, so much so that a string of negative events would arise, leading him further down this trail of misery. I remember telling him, "Tre, it's okay. Let it go. Stop focusing on it. It's over." Instead, he would wallow in his misery, supporting this lie that he was telling himself, that he and the team "sucked." What happened? Circumstances showed up to support this "suckey" attitude. I had to get him to learn to finally stop feeling and believing the negative talk in his head and start focusing on positive things.

We worked on his "I Am" statements, and he started releasing a more powerful version of himself. He changed his focus and found a few positive statements that he could magnify, with his energy squarely focused on his goal, and those things began to manifest. He started believing in himself and working harder on the things that he was good at. He stopped worrying about the things he couldn't change. He started taking responsibility and began investing in the many great qualities he had. Workouts turned into two-a-days. We hired a specialized speed training coach. He deepened his faith through prayer. He started congratulating and praising his team, and he began to see a new outcome for himself. He kept his eyes on his future, despite what was showing up in the present. He trusted God's plan for him and allowed the great forces of the universe to guide and direct his actions. Tre will tell you that in one summer, he went from believing he "sucked" to knowing himself as a "superstar." Superstars and superstar teams win football games.

If you don't see yourself as a superstar, nobody else will, including the other team. Your competition will pounce all over you.

Believe in yourself. Love and accept who you are. Embrace your limited abilities, and put your focus on what you can do well and what you are willing to improve on.

Whatever you are giving attention to, whatever you are thinking about, feeling, focusing on, talking about, even trying not to think about, it will show up in your life. It's the law of attraction: like attracts like.

You are sending out your energy, and the universe responds by sending you a like energy. If you don't believe that your dream is possible, then no one else will, and forces in the universe will align with this disbelief.

You have to be so focused and committed to your passion and dream, taking full responsibility for what is showing up in your life and what you are attracting.

Successful people focus on what they want and take responsibility for making it happen. They also take responsibility for not making it happen. Being responsible liberates you. It lets you freely acknowledge the successes you've achieved and the failures you've experienced. When you don't take responsibility, you are giving away your power. In order to keep your life-reins solidly in the palm of your hands, you must take and retain full responsibility for everything you are doing, believing, and experiencing.

Negative and difficult things happen to every one of us. Some of it is completely out of our control, but how we react and respond, how we view the conditions and circumstances around us, and what level of responsibility we take, is totally up to us.

The amount of negative energy we give to the problem or condition will greatly impact how it affects us in the days and weeks to come, simply because we get what we focus on.

ACTION PLAN

We all have to find ways to step back, smell the roses and be grateful for where we are and what we have. Finding and keeping balance is an important process in reaching your goals and dreams. Answer the questions below in order to measure your work-life balance.

QUESTIONS

1. What ways can you find to relax and unplug?
2. What are three small things you really enjoying doing that deserve your attention or that you can celebrate?
3. What do you love the most about yourself?
4. What area of your life deserves more attention, and what action can you take today to change that?

HUSTLE TIP

"If you want a recipe for how to hustle, just go out and do it. What is the worst thing that could happen? Someone tells you no? Here's a thought, it's just no for now."

- LaShanda Henry, Founder of SistaSense.com, website developer and internet marketer - *Hustle & Heart TV* on Episode 12

HEART TIP

"When you think about your business from the heart perspective, you have to say to yourself 'why am I doing this' because if you don't have a clear reason why, when you feel drained or you're lacking motivation it's easy to stop, it's easy to turn course, so just do it and make sure you know why you're doing it."

- LaShanda Henry, Founder of SistaSense.com, website developer and internet marketer - *Hustle & Heart TV* on Episode 12

CHAPTER SEVEN
ABUNDANCE AND FLOW

Faith in God, the Universe, and Infinite Possibilities

You can see the law of attraction everywhere. You draw
everything to yourself. The people, the job, the circumstances,
the health, the wealth, the debt, the joy, the car that you drive,
the community that you're in. And you've drawn them all to you,
like a magnet. What you think about, you bring about.
Your whole life is a manifestation of the thoughts
that go on in your head.

-Lisa Nichols-

The fabric of your life is stitched together by the cumulative consequences of your choices, millions of them, made every second of your life. When you act, react, believe, perceive, disbelief, or misperceive, you are steered in a certain direction. If you are dissatisfied with life and your choices, take full responsibility for what is happening. You can blame *yourself* for the blanket of circumstances covering you.

You are exactly where you decide and choose to be. You can choose to be wealthy or choose to be poor. It's all up to you, your mindset, your belief system, and what you are focusing on. You can choose to align your life with greater purpose or choose the actions that dictate your life. You can choose to believe these theories or choose not to. The common denominator is you.

Thankfully, I believe no matter what we choose, we are all supported by a magnificent God and Creator, by an ever-flowing universe of opportunities, and by a divine process of creation. We can change our circumstances by changing our choices.

Your financial situations are no exception. If you are aware of the law of attraction and the principle of flowing energy, then most of this should sound familiar to you. If you are not aware of the law of attraction, this chapter will begin to explore the profound concepts of like attracting like and getting what you focus on.

Your ability to choose is the most powerful control you have in your life. Clearly I understand that people don't choose to be poor, sick, or live in undesirable situations. However, sometimes people make poor decisions that slowly assemble into a poor set of circumstances. Retrace the footsteps to poverty and despair. It happens slowly, systematically, consistently, and methodically under the steady guise of poor choices. To make matters worse, when we see poor conditions start to emerge in our life and we focus on it, we attract even more poor conditions.

Recognize that every day, you make decisions that will have a ripple effect throughout your future. The question is this: will your choice create a wave of happiness and wealth or depression and poverty?

It's time to start practicing abundance and flow.

Esteemed speaker, author, and life coach Lisa Nichols was a struggling single mother on public assistance in South Central

Los Angeles, who found her hustle and is now a millionaire entrepreneur. She has made it her mission to teach others how to change their lives using the power of transformative thought.

The world first came to know her as a featured teacher in The Secret, a popular book and film in the mid-2000s based on the law of attraction. She is a living testimony of its power.

The law of attraction states that "like attracts like," so when you think a thought, you are also attracting like thoughts to you.

Thoughts are sticky. They are like magnets and have a frequency. As you think thoughts, you're sending them out into the universe, and they are attracting all other like things that are vibrating on the same frequency.

Your current thoughts are creating your future life. What you think and focus on the most will appear in your life. Nothing can come into your experience unless you summon it through persistent thoughts. If you are thinking of abundance, prosperity, joy, and happiness, and you are flowing that steady stream of good, positive energy, you will attract that in return.

I know many people think this sounds mystical, displaced, and unimaginable. However, the fact remains: it is a law of the universe, and this law is always present, whether we choose to believe it or not. The law of attraction is always at work.

ASK

You get to choose what you want, but you must be clear about it. You must feel strongly about having it. That's why passion is so powerful; it creates a wave of energy, emotions, and feelings that, with the law of attraction, can produce amazing results.

If you're not clear about what you're thinking, how you're feeling, and what you are asking for, you will send mixed signals and only attract mixed or poor results.

Choosing is asking. Asking is the first step in the creative process that initiates the law of attraction. Get into the habit of asking the universe for what you want.

BELIEVE

You must have complete and unwavering faith that what you have asked for is already yours.

Believing in the unseen and trusting in a process that always delivers is important to your success. The moment you make a choice and ask, the process of creation begins. How it will happen, how this law of attraction works, and how the universe will answer what you've asked for is not your concern. Allow the unfolding to begin. When you are trying to figure out how it will happen, you are emitting a frequency that contains a lack of faith and belief, which completely halts the process. You think you have to do it all, and you do not believe the universe can do it for you. You begin to set up doubt and worry, thus blocking all of your blessings.

How do you get yourself to believe this? It's having faith in the unseen. Some, myself included would say it's having faith in a power and presence greater than you. Your belief that you will have what you want and your undying faith are your greatest power, your greatest assets to attracting what you want and need. You must do the work, and trust completely in this process for the flow of abundance to begin pouring into your life.

RECEIVE

Receiving is the last step in the process of the law of attraction. Receiving is accepting with a sense of knowing. It's also important to feel the emotions of being in receipt of something. It's important to feel good and to emote a type of energy that pulls in a higher frequency. Get yourself to a feel-good place and start attracting and vibrating at higher levels to receive more quickly.

Seriously, start imagining yourself becoming, doing, having, and experiencing all of those things that you've been dreaming about. Take that burning passion, fire, and desire and turn it up several notches. Get excited about having what you want, as if it is happening right now. Get physical and emotional. Engage all of your senses around actually receiving what it is you are asking for. When you do this, you start to engage the higher vibrations in the universe, speeding up the process of receiving. Amazingly, it almost works in reverse. When you feel as though you have what it is you're dreaming about right now, and the feeling is so real, you are intensifying the creation process, and flow begins to happen.

You are a magnet, attracting everything to you by your thoughts, emotions, and actions. When you are clear in your mind about what you want, you immediately begin to draw those things to you. The more you practice and begin to see the law of attraction working, the greater magnet you can become.

Trust your instincts. Your instincts can help you create a definitive outline in this process. It's the knowing that you are being inspired that helps the process progress. Your instincts are the universe communicating with you, letting you know, in an intuitive and instinctive way, to continue to engage in this feel-good energy. Follow it and allow it to flow to you.

Everything that has been invented and created on this planet came from one thought. That one thought came from some man or woman who, with a great sense of passion, decided and declared that they would give birth to their invention. That thought or choice was the seed planted. Through belief and hard work, those inventions evolved. Your passion and your dreams are no different. They too can manifest from the invisible to the visible. Trust this process. Have faith and allow the universe to work. Enjoy the outcome.

Focus on sending out into the universe strong feelings of joy and happiness. When you do that, you will attract all of the things that bring you joy and happiness. These things include running a successful business, making the kind of money that you want, creating powerful relationships, enjoying a healthy lifestyle, and so much more. You must radiate a clear description of what you want brought back to you. The law of attraction is reflecting back your deepest thoughts and emotions. You simply have to ask, believe, and then receive. Leave the how to the universe.

If you come from a place of lack and scarcity, and are focused on lack and scarcity, you'll get more of that. I know it's hard to think about having something that you don't already have. Believe that it is going to somehow come into your life, especially if this is your first understanding of the law of attraction. It's been working in your life all along, although you may have been unaware of it. This method of creation is always occurring. You can learn to manifest the abundance you desire in your life by always being aware of this and learning to only radiate good positive feelings.

In the case of money, you have to feel good about attracting more of it to you.

Understandably, when people do not have enough money, they don't feel good even talking about the subject. However, those negative feelings about not having enough money are stopping more money from coming to you. You have to stop the cycle. You stop it by starting to feel good about money and being grateful for what you do have. Start to say and feel you are abundantly blessed. This is the mantra I use as part of my "I Am" statements:

"There is more than enough. There are constant streams of income steadily flowing to me. I am attracting everything that I need to be successful right now. I am a money magnet. I love money, and money loves me. I am grateful for all that I am and for all that I am becoming."

Now if you can take this a step further and start feeling good about giving money away and blessing others with it, you can turn up the power to attract what you need. As you demonstrate the faith of giving, the law of attraction must give you more to give.

Prosperity is your birthright, and you are deserving of abundance, freedom, and possibility. You deserve every good thing you want, and God and the Universe will give you those desires as you summon them into your life. Are you open to great abundance and flow from the universe?

ACTION PLAN

Write your answers to the following questions:

QUESTIONS

1. What are you asking for?
2. Do you truly believe this is possible?
3. Do you get emotionally charged and excited when you see yourself accomplishing your dream and goals?
4. Do you love what you're doing?
5. Do you love providing the product, service, or whatever it is that you are bringing to the marketplace with your business?

HUSTLE TIP

"The tip is just keep going. You don't quit—that's it. Keep your hustle when you're driving and figure out what you want…Is it your kids, your husband, your wife, your family? Do you want to get them a new home? What is it that you want and go after it, and don't let anybody tell you can't, because you can?"

- Troy Miles, Owner, The Miles Group of Lincoln Heritage Insurance - *Hustle & Heart TV* on Episode 1

HEART TIP

"Embrace it, embrace that journey."

- Troy Miles, Owner, The Miles Group of Lincoln Heritage Insurance - *Hustle & Heart TV* on Episode 1

CHAPTER EIGHT
DEFINED ACTION PLANS

Time, Money, Systems and Help

Is it your desire to become financially independent?
Then act like it. Actions are what will make your dreams
come to life. The actions you take will create the reality of
your life. Those people who have achieved financial
independence have done so by acting in a certain way.
You can do the same. Wishing will not make it so.
Complaining will not make it so. Your actions will make it so.
Every moment of every day you have the opportunity to mold
your life by virtue of the actions you take.

-Les Brown-

We are living in the greatest age of self-discovery, self-advancement, and wealth creation. You could be the next kitchen table business sensation!

You will need to decide right now that you will purposely find ways to turn what you love doing, what you know you are good at, what you are so passionate about, into streams of income. If your passion is already tied to a structured system, a franchise, network marketing company, or a powerful compensation plan, perfect; you are more than halfway there.

Work that system, duplicate success, don't reinvent the wheel, and plug as many people, resources, and opportunities into place as possible.

Turn up your hustle. Get really jazzed about marketing and selling your product or service. Don't deviate from the plan, and be focused on helping and serving as many people as possible.

There are thousands of ways to make money. There is a ton of information out there to teach you how. There are enough books, tapes, programs, coaches, and courses available about how to create extra income. Go out and find, purchase and use them. However, we all know if all we needed was more information, everyone with an Internet connection would live in a mansions, drive expensive cars, take long vacations, and live happily ever after. We are consistently hit with sensational claims on how to get rich quick, make $500,000 a year working seven hours a week, or find lasting success in some half-baked scheme.

It appears to me that giving you more information about specific systems and programs is not what you need (although I'm happy to refer you to a few of the ones that I have been successfully using). Becoming a distributor with It Works! Global and marketing those "Crazy Wraps" made me a huge amount of money over a short period of time. Plus I was able to leverage successful tools and systems for a mere few hundred dollars a month in operating expenses. Network marketing is a tremendously viable system and vehicle for success, and me leading a team of distributors all following a series of steps was paramount to my success. If developing multiple streams of income is important to you, then I would strongly encourage you, as part of one of those streams, to consider joining a solid, successful network marketing company with cutting edge products and services, a strong track record of success, and whose leaders have integrity and long range vision.

Let's focus on creating new behaviors and habits for when you find that perfect company or for when you begin to create your perfect system of success. Let's explore how your behaviors align with your passions. Then it will come natural for you to choose to create or take part in vehicles and opportunities to create multiple streams of income. You'll be hitching your passion to systems and businesses that serve you, in turn allowing you to create greater influence and leveraging you in the direction of success.

CONSISTENT ACTION

The first behavior we will look at is taking consistent daily action.

When you set a course for achieving your goal, you should also set up measurable steps that you plan out and can track daily, weekly, monthly, and yearly. You should be able to set up a predictable and manageable timetable that allows you to review whether you're actively moving closer to achieving your goal. We sometimes get this twisted, and think that we can jump from point A to point Z with little time or effort. We start off believing that it will take much hard work, strategic planning, money, and time, then we mistakenly set a course without actively accounting for these resources. This is a dreadful blunder. Earning success is hard. The process is tedious, laborious, boring, and often takes much longer than expected. Becoming influential and a world-class entrepreneur is slow and difficult. This explains why there's generally so much distance from the 5 percent at the top and the masses that occupy the other 95 percent.

If you have an aversion to hard work, commitment, and discipline, you're welcome to put this book down and walk away from creating profit streams from your passion. This would all be just a waste of your time.

Change happens because of a series of small and smart choices that are consistently made to reap a benefit. This is so surprising to most people because they never see the small, seemingly insignificant, consistent action-steps that lead to the major successes. Instead, they concentrate on the big payoff at the end, while giving little consideration to the painstaking small actions that compound daily to build positive momentum toward the end goal.

If you've ever been on a diet, then you can relate to this. You start off with a goal of losing ten to twenty pounds. You throw out all the bad food and bring in all the good stuff. You buy new workout gear and, once again, finally commit to shedding those excess pounds. The first few days go fabulous, but when you step on the scale and notice only a slight change, you become discouraged. Change didn't happen fast enough. You don't prepare yourself for just how long it is really going to take to lose those pounds, and you think you should go from fat to thin in a matter of days.

You must get it in your head and heart that you need to remain focused and be consistent as you move closer to accomplishing your chosen outcome. As a result, you are likely to remain on course longer and stay more involved with the daily tasks. This can even become enjoyable once we realize just how simple the phenomenal power of consistent daily action can be.

The difference is obvious between people who employ consistency for their benefit compared with those who don't take action daily toward the same goal. It is especially discernible at the completion of the objective when one person thrives and the other withers. It almost looks miraculous, like magic or luck. What's really happened is that consistent action, compounded over time, equals the so-called overnight success.

Don't have a microwave mentality when achieving your goals. The good old-fashioned process of putting something in the oven and letting it bake for its proper amount of time is the best way to ensure a tasty result. The only path to success is through a continuum of sometimes unexciting, mundane, challenging, *daily* disciplines carried out over time. The compound effect is a law, and it's certain and unavoidable: every action or inaction compounds over time.

When we know this, we can begin to take the necessary steps toward our dream. We can start to do the math, add this up, and take score. If it's important to your success that you make "X" amount of calls or contact "X" amount of people, I bet there's an average that equals a certain result.

Once you know this, be consistent at doing the daily tasks. The results will begin to show up. Just the same, if you do nothing each day, then the resulting payoff is nothing.

BECOME AN EXPERT
AT YOUR PASSION

Think of becoming an expert at what you are passionate about. Experts can offer detailed how-to information that solves problems, offers solutions, and supports the success of others. As an expert you can communicate your knowledge with informational products sold on and offline such as videos, audios, blogs, and other courses that provide a proven outcome or result. You may choose to communicate your expertise by speaking, holding workshops, collaborating with others, or doing webinars and web based trainings or seminars and workshops. You could even set up one-on-one and group meetings to share what you know and love.

You can get extremely creative with ways that you can package what you know and love. Make a goal of supporting others with your knowledge by helping them to find solutions to their problems and guiding them to a more successful result.

Find your niche and your avatar, then stay focused on serving that community.

INVEST IN YOURSELF

You can't do this alone. You will need someone to show and guide you along your journey. The sooner you make it a point to invest in a good coach or mentor, the faster you'll see results.

Coaches and experts in your field can help you mitigate the unavoidable challenges you will face. Their guidance is intended to save you time and money. Plus you could easily model their success. A coach sees in you what you don't see in yourself. They can help you in many ways. Consider finding someone in your field and working closely with them, either in a coaching or mentoring relationship.

You will also want to invest in systems and trainings. With the amount of tools and information available to start, grow, and expand a business, you will not have a hard time finding the right product that matches your business goals. Attend trainings. Get the right books and online programs. Automate your processes. Find ways to streamline your operations through software systems.

You should be spending your time doing the highest income producing activity available to you. Find ways to outsource those other things that are necessary but pull you away from making money.

Your two biggest investments are in yourself and in others.

BUILD A TEAM

Get some help. Whether it's a partner, a family member, a friend, or a virtual assistant, you will need people around you can trust.

The sooner you determine your chief role and figure out how to get help with the other things, the better. If money is tight, ask for volunteers, get college students, or create an internship or apprenticeship. If you are a creating a product or service, and there is available money when that product or service is sold, create a profit sharing program. Agree to give your team a percentage of each sale. You can come up with creative ways to compensate people for their time and commitment.

DON'T WASTE ENERGY

Time and money are exchanges of energy. They are either wasted or flow into your life with synergy. With money, you either attract a lot of it or a little of it, depending on how your energy is flowing. You are either attracting opportunities to make more money or repelling those opportunities.

It takes a massive mind shift to move from being broke to attracting sources of income, then to making money and making enough of it to be financially free. It's a process that starts with your belief and mindset. You'll never move away from being broke if you don't shift your mind to believing that you can create sources of income. It is living in the knowledge that you will attract the right opportunities, the right people, the right circumstances, and the right outcomes that attract these things into your life.

Visualize how your passions will serve others. You must be clearly able to see your money flowing to you.

A passion-inspired and successful entrepreneur assumes the following attitude: They *set* goals, and not just random goals— they have intent and purpose, with deadlines and objectives. They can be measured, monitored, adjusted, and controlled.

Do you remember the piece of advice I shared earlier? To better hold yourself accountable to achieving your goal, try aligning your goal with your "why." We can easily get off track and set goals that don't mirror our "why." We know that we are off track whenever we carry out the goal but it doesn't satisfy the "why." Make sure your goals mirror your "why."

Be flexible, be steadfast in your pursuit, be accountable, be responsible, be honest, and be forthright about the goals that you have.

Have you set any new goals recently? Have you dusted off the ones that were important to you a couple of months or couple of years ago to see if they are still valid?

If you haven't determined your "why" and set a few goals, find some quiet time over the next couple of days to get centered, focused, and do some reflection. Write them down and put them in places that will remind you every day *why* you are hustling for your dreams.

The passion-inspired and successful entrepreneur is also *not afraid to fail.* That doesn't mean that they don't have fears or doubts; it simply means they go after their goals with courage and bravery. In fact, fearless entrepreneurs invite failure. Many of my guests on *Hustle & Heart TV* have told me that they only know that they are closer to achieving their goals by the number of times they failed in their attempts to reach them.

You have to be okay with failing. Your success and failure are only measurable by your own standards, which are your goals and your "why." Failing is oftentimes just a part of the process.

Anything in life worth having presents us with ups and downs. There is good and bad, there is light and dark, there is an ebb and flow in every birthing process. There is always the opposite end of the spectrum. There is always another way and another day to get things right-side up again. Embrace your failed attempts. There is a lesson in everything; there is even a lesson in failure.

The passion-inspired and successful entrepreneur *puts systems into place and builds teams.* Would you describe yourself as a type A, driven, do-it-yourself personality? Do you have the Superwoman/Superman syndrome? Do you possess the arrogance that you can do it all and do it all by yourself? Many times I oscillate in and out of this weird place of always being in control.

Here's a reality check: we can do anything, we just can't do *everything.* Even sometimes in doing anything, we need help. We have to learn to ask for help. We have to put systems into place and create a supportive network around us. Whether it's your employees, your friends and family, some colleagues, or a mastermind group, chances are you'll need some help. If you're going to be a titan in your industry, a seven-figure success, an Internet guru, a top-notch chef, the bomb.com, or a rock star in whatever you're doing, you'll need to be a leader, and you'll need a team. You need to be a leader who's not afraid of asking for help and leveraging systems in order to lead. I'm reminded of the saying, "It takes a village to raise a child." Well, it takes a team to raise a leader, and the sooner you build a team around you, the more effective you can be as a leader.

Leaders come in all shapes and sizes. Heck, if you are a parent with kids, you are leading. Certainly in business we have to see ourselves as leaders. So I must ask you…what systems do you have in place to support you? What automation, tools, and processes do you have working for you that allow you to stay focused on your "why," get closer to achieving your goals, help you mitigate the chances of failure, and support you as an effective leader?

What does your system look like around you? What can you begin to incorporate today that will automate and streamline what you're doing? Is there someone else that you can ask for help? Can you find interns or contractors to help provide additional service or resources?

There are plenty of ways for you to look for a support system and to build a team around you. In today's world of technology, most of it can be virtual or online. Just know that highly successful entrepreneurs rely on systems and teams to be and become successful.

I can tell you that former Pittsburgh Steeler and successful entrepreneur Chuck Sanders of Savoy Restaurant and Urban Lending definitely has systems and a strong team in place. Restaurant titan Pat McDonnell of Atria's, Juniper Grill, and Ditka's restaurants, who has also had a hand in developing some eighty restaurants, did not get to where he is without systems and a team around him. Want more advice around building teams? Watch their episodes on Hustle & Heart TV at *www.HustleandHeartTV.com.*

Finally, the passion-inspired and successful entrepreneur *hustles*. They work hard, grind, and put the pedal to the metal. We are talking about the kind of hustle that exhausts most people around them and elevates them to the top 5 percent in the industry they are dominating. Hustle is the thing that sets the extremely successful people apart from the majority. Successful entrepreneurs hustle like there's no tomorrow. At every attempt, they give it their all, all of their attention, focus, energy, and commitment. Hustlers are not afraid to fail, they're not afraid to go after what they want in spite of their doubts or the naysayers. They are shameless and not bashful about their work ethic.

Are you a hustler? If so, welcome to your tribe.

ACTION PLAN

Challenge yourself over the next thirty days to create a new plan of consistent action around two areas of your life: business/career, family/relationships.

QUESTIONS

Write your answers to the following questions:

1. What bad habits are you consistently doing that you know are derailing you from your success?
2. What are you avoiding that you know, if you acted on consistently, could begin to make improvements in your life?
3. What do you see yourself having in direct proportion to how you are expressing, utilizing, and leveraging your passions?
4. What do you see others doing that you could easily do if you only took a chance, the time, and then modeled it?
5. How can you collaborate and partner to create joint ventures and affiliates with others?

Make a list of your highest income producing activities. Begin to offload or redirect to your staff any activities that are time wasters for you. You know what they are!

HUSTLE TIP

"Do the basics, most people won't even do the basics to get started. I continue, I call it Thank you Thursdays, I hand write, not any other service, you actually sit down and hand write thank you cards to people who have helped you."

- Becky Auer, Marketing Coach, Speaker and Author - *Hustle & Heart TV* on Episode 19

HEART TIP

"You have to love what you are doing. My passion is marketing, doing those direct mail campaigns, I love that, I love being unique and different with my groups and showing ways to position yourself as the expert and all of those things that you need to do. If you don't love what you're doing, you're in the wrong business."

- Becky Auer, Marketing Coach, Speaker and Author - *Hustle & Heart TV* on Episode 19

CHAPTER NINE

GIVE VALUE AND SERVICE

A Mission to Serve Others

Make your customers comfortable and
they will give you their lives.

-Paul Orfalea-

Paul Orfalea, the founder of Kinko's, took life's challenges and used them to propel himself into an unforeseeable future. Paul was a struggling kid who could barely read or write who suffered with dyslexia and ADHD. He took his perceived disabilities and created a compassionate work atmosphere that garnered his company Fortune Magazine's designation of being one of the best places in America to work. He not only mastered pleasing his employees but also his customers with the same philosophy, to the tune of $1.5 billion in the early 2000s.

He is a prime example of how turning your passions into profit means taking what you love and know and providing it as a product or service for others. When you can match your talents, your gifts, and what you are passionate about doing with the needs and wants of others, then you have a formula for success. You bring value to them in ways that support their desires.

I'm excited we are on this journey together! There is no better time than right now to bring value and service to the world. You can take your passion and become the go-to expert in your niche market. The world is always searching for a better way, a faster, more effective approach to doing things, a different and unique approach to old problems. The Internet has made it possible for people to connect with experts on any subject in a matter of seconds. Become that go-to person, and it instantaneously increases your ability to make money and create a successful outcome, especially if you are also helping others in the process.

Helping others is not passé as some would have you think. It is the bedrock of every successful society. Most of us learned the Golden Rule when we were in grade school. It is based on the idea that people should treat others in the same way that they themselves would like to be treated. This also translates into entrepreneurship. Your customers, both internal and external, want to be treated the same way that you would like to be treated if you were in their shoes. Your internal clients are your employees, vendors, and contractors. It's virtually anybody that is on your dream support team. Your external clients are your customers who buy goods, services, and products from you.

The old adage "The customer is always right" is still relevant in customer relations for small business owners, especially in today's competitive market. Jason Nazar, author of *16 Surprising Statistics about Small Businesses*, states that "approximately

543,000 new businesses get started each month (but more employer businesses shut down than start up each month)."[1]

As you are striving to reach your individual goals as an entrepreneur, you can't forget about serving those who co-labor with you on the track to your success. You must value your employees, interns, helpers, and volunteers because they help fuel your vision.

I have had great success in multilevel and network marketing because I cherished the art of team building and goal setting. Everyone has a "why"—I made it my aim to know what that was for each member of my team so we all could cross the finish line of success. I also made it a priority to provide them with the necessary tools and training to get the job done. I wasn't satisfied with me being the only cheerleader for our cause. I made sure that everyone was cheering each other on by keeping their visions before them and reminding them of their "why."

You must also value building better customer relationships because this can make or break your business. Word of mouth advertising is one of the most effective ways to build your business, and all it costs you is great customer service delivery. When I opened Fullbody Fitness Club in 2011, I counted the cost of introducing a new concept of fitness into the exercise market. We had the first aerial fitness program of its kind in Pittsburgh. Remember, I love taking an idea and watching it grow and take flight (pun intended)! I was energized by the mere notion of starting a new venture, and my enthusiasm was contagious. I dreamed incessantly about pulling this off, and I started finding what I needed in instructors, resources,

---

1. *http://www.forbes.com/sites/jasonnazar/2013/09/09/16-surprising-statistics-about-small-businesses/*

and partnerships. I employed all of the strategies I've been sharing with you in this book; I planned, worked hard, made connections, dreamed big, stated "I Am" affirmations, let go of the fears and doubts, and allowed the universe to flow back to me exactly what I needed.

Even more exciting things began to happen. Fullbody Fitness Club was also one of the few fitness studios in the United States to partner with entertainment sensation Cirque du Soleil and sports giant Reebok to unveil their unique fitness programs, Jukari *Fit to Fly* and Jukari *Fit to Flex*. I was so excited when I inked the deal to bring this to Pittsburgh! We could count ourselves as a unique fitness playground with classes like aerial yoga, aerial silk dance, ballet barre, pole dance, Zumba, and so much more.

We had a lot to offer, but our potential clients needed to be aware of what we offered and how these somewhat intimidating classes would benefit their physical, mental, and spiritual health. Our slogan, "Transform Your Workout, Awaken Your Spirit," told our story, but our existing clients had to validate our marketing promises with word-of-mouth advertising in order for us to get more customers. We also had to deliver excellent customer service consistently as promised. We did so with a smile, regardless of whether we had a few people in a class or forty. My incredible team of instructors always gave their best workouts, no matter the attendance. Because of that, we built a loyal following and a unique brand.

Here are a few tips on how to provide value to your customers even when business is slow:

1. Do the unexpected.
2. Deliver good customer service.
3. Under-promise and over-deliver.
4. Set manageable expectations and "wow" them when you do more than they expected.
5. Give your customers tokens of your appreciation.
6. Tailor your advertising content to be user friendly on your virtual communications such as your website, emails, and social media posts.
7. Be personal!
8. Don't just give them what they paid for. Provide informational products that are customer centered, that add more value to your products, goods, or services. For example, you could provide white papers, blog posts, and e-books to build your customer relations.
9. Periodically ask them what they want through customer surveys and customer focus groups.
10. Help your customers succeed by actually talking with them about their goals and objectives related to the products or services you offer.

Keeping the customers' "why" a priority in your business strategy means more money in your bank account. Hustle to make it happen with each customer and watch your bottom line increase exponentially as a result!

I sold Fullbody Fitness Club in October of 2014 to two of my aerialists. That experience is part of what spawned this book. I'm so grateful for the journey I enjoyed with our customers, members, and my instructors. It was priceless and well worth the experience. The sale afforded me the opportunity to take some of the proceeds and donate them to charities I support.

Earlier I talked a little about Paul Orfalea, the founder of Kinko's. Well, in 2004 he sold Kinko's to FedEx Corporation and has since become a philanthropist. He didn't stop helping people, because his passion is people. He matched his passion with the needs and wants of others, which explains his continued success as an entrepreneur.

As a small business owner, giving is important. You may think that it's impossible for you to give in this economy, so below are some tips that will empower you to give without breaking your bank or filing for bankruptcy while still increasing your business's exposure. Holly Hall, an editor at "Chronicle of Philanthropy" states, "More and more businesses are waking up to the fact they want to have a charitable tie-in that makes sense for their business and helps their bottom line." When you or your company gives and donates time and money, you are not only helping and supporting your cause, you are also potentially increasing your influence and customer loyalty. You can use your giving as a marketing campaign…and you don't have to always give cash. You can donate free or discounted products, or volunteer your time or that of your employees.

Be strategic when you identify causes or nonprofits that you want to give to. Here's a roadmap to help you make the best choice for your business:

1. Look at your company's vision statement and determine what cause would be a good fit for your organization.
2. Make the decision a company decision. Ask for feedback from your employees.
3. Do a thorough investigation of the organizations that you may want to partner with.
4. Determine what you would like to contribute without it crippling your business.
5. Let your customers know that you are supporting your community; they may want to get involved. You may be helping someone find the vehicle they had been looking for to fulfill their passion.

Remember, in all of your giving, make value and service the trademark of your actions.

THE SERVANT-LEADER

Bringing value to the marketplace can happen when you take your service to the next level: servant leadership.

The phrase "servant-leadership" was first found in an essay in 1970 by Robert K. Greenleaf titled, "The Servant as Leader." The philosophy behind the phrase puts serving others first. A servant-leader focuses on growing the individuals, companies, communities, and nations to which they belong. Greenleaf says the best test of this concept is when we can answer the following questions affirmatively:

- Do those served grow as persons?
- Do they, while being served, become healthier, wiser, freer, more autonomous, more likely themselves to become servants?
- What is the effect on the least privileged in society?
- Will they benefit or at least not be further deprived?

A servant-leader shares power, is instrumental in the growth of others, and literally makes it their aim to help others achieve their higher good. As a hustler after your dreams, it is your responsibility to model servant-leadership in your sphere of influence. Wealth begets power, and power used to serve others makes this world a better place to live in. Get your hustle on as a servant-leader!

ACTION PLAN

To better identify if your passions are aligned with helping others, answer these questions:

QUESTIONS

1. How can your passion help others toward a better personal or professional life?
2. How will your skills allow you to solve other people's problems?
3. Are there others doing what you are passionate about and experiencing successful outcomes?
4. Can you easily model or duplicate someone who is already successful doing what you love, but then also add your special touch or flare?

HUSTLE TIP

"Being honest with yourself, know how best you market yourself. If you're a talker, be a talker, if you're a schmoozer, be a schmoozer, do what you have to do. Figure out your own formula."

- Chuck Sanders, CEO of Urban Lending Solutions and Owner of Savoy Restaurant - *Hustle & Heart TV* on Episode 17

HEART TIP

"If you're going to talk about entrepreneurship, and if you're going to talk about building a business, then have a goal that's bigger than everything. For me it's just generational wealth. Doing it for the money, for the accolades, it fades very quickly. There has to be such a passion, for me its legacy, for someone else, I think you're fooling yourself if you think it's for money. Even if you make the money or don't make the money you get to a point where, you have to wake up every day and really be fired up about this. If you're not fired up and have a passion to win and do this you're not gonna have what it take to have the hustle to get it done."

- Chuck Sanders, CEO of Urban Lending Solutions and Owner of Savoy Restaurant - *Hustle & Heart TV* on Episode 17

CHAPTER TEN

HUSTLE

Ready to Go

"Things may come to those who wait...
but only the things left by those who hustle."

-Abraham Lincoln-

President Abraham Lincoln had the right idea when he made this statement in the 18th century. Hustlers create the tidal wave, they don't flow with it! Advance without hesitation. Be bold, be brave, be fierce, and stay focused on your destination.

New York Times bestselling author Jon Acuff, author of *Start: Punch Fear in the Face, Escape Average & Do Work that Matters*, knows a little something about hustling. If you want to master the art of the hustle, you must "punch fear in the face, escape average, and do work that matters." It is under your control, so take that leap of faith and soar into your greatness. In other words, now is your time to hustle. "I want the peace in knowing that it wasn't for lack of hustling that I missed a target for my dream," Acuff says. "I want to know that the one thing in my control was under control."

You must never tire of your hustle. Although exhausted and sometimes weathered and worn, what you intend for your life will show up as a result of all of your hustle and your consistency.

Remember, you are not the sum of your intentions but the sum of your actions. The urgency and the speed at which you go after your passions will always keep you energized and ready for whatever life has to offer. Hustling is about taking action *before* the perfect conditions arise, taking a leap of faith before we receive permission, stepping out before it appears reasonable, and moving forward before others anticipate your next move.

Choosing your own aim and seeking to bring it to fulfillment with a sense of purpose and passion creates an unstoppable energy. We will have made nothing of ourselves or created anything significant unless we are prepared to hustle and take action, *now*.

What skills do you need? Acquire them now. What tools do you require? Put hands on them now. What resources will support you? Discover them now. Who will need to join you? Find them now. What sacrifices do you need to make? Do it now.

Be honest and brave in assessing your life and ask yourself: How hard am I really working toward my dream? Am I letting little obstacles stop my progress, or am I battling through them on a consistent basis? Am I acting with real conviction and commitment in life, or simply trudging through it? Have I struggled to succeed in any area of my life because I failed to sacrifice or commit?

If we have real dreams, then we must hustle for them. For the sake of our soul and our happiness, we must remain hungry, ambitious, and courageous.

When you are squarely committed to seeing your passion through to the realization of a dream, there is little time to waste. You cannot afford to grow tired or stall. You must commit to fighting harder and longer when moving toward your dreams. Spend some time writing down all the things you have been wanting to do, along with all of the excuses for not doing them. Contemplate where you're being weak or progressing too slowly. Figure out what obstacles you have been allowing to stop you and decide to get past them and move forward.

THERE IS NO SUBSTITUTE FOR HARD WORK

Greatness isn't handed to anyone; it requires a lot of hard work. Yet we all know that isn't enough, since many people work hard for decades without approaching greatness or even getting significantly better.

You will also need all of the things we explored in this book: passion, purpose, clearly defined goals, an action plan, and an unstoppable and unshakable "why."

Tiger Woods, Michael Jordan, and Usane Bolt are great examples of athletes that are exceptional and reached the top of their chosen field. They got there by devoting countless hours to practice and hustle. Consistently working hard kept them at the top of their game and allowed them to outpace their competition. Constantly practicing an activity improves performance. It involves high levels of repetition and provides an athlete with increased feedback on results and performance. In essence, consistent practice equals better performance, and with copious amounts, it equals exceptional performance.

For us common folks, who are not physically gifted like my aforementioned phenoms, we can still apply the same amount of hustle to our daily business activities and reap successful results.

KEEP THE PRESSURE ON

Exceptional athletes know they must perform when the pressure is on, as they constantly place pressure on themselves to always be prepared to win.

Take a leaf out of their book on success and apply some pressure to your hustle. Learn to push yourself harder and be shameless about expecting your ultimate success. Strive for excellence in everything you do. Exceed expectations. Never be content with good when you know with a little more effort you can go for great. When you strive for excellence in everything you do, you will naturally surpass others and reach your true potential.

My greatest wish for you is that you will discover that your passions do have purpose, that you can find them, share them, give them to the world, and earn money in the process. Along this journey of self-discovery and profiting, my hope is that you will also love the process. Perhaps loving your journey is the most important aspect of all of this. It can be grueling work to hustle for your passion, to work hard, to put in long hours, pour sweat and tears and end short of your achievement. I have been there and done that many times, though never discouraged. Hustling doesn't have to be a non-enjoyable experience. You can love your journey, and you can lead a lifestyle full of opportunity and abundance every day.

We all have a story, a message, a skill, a talent, and a gift that has and will inspire others. Let me encourage you again to turn your passions into profit, and of course to do this you will need to hustle. In business, you must share this passion in innovative ways that quickly sets you apart from the competition. You will need good business sense and an entrepreneurial mindset to turn those passions into profit. You will need to stand out, stand up, stand forward, and stand ready to employ practical business skills, leverage connections and contacts, and proven business strategies to make it. You don't have to reinvent the wheel, you just have to turn off cruise control, hit the gas, and put the pedal to the metal.

To turn your passions into profit, you must fill the needs and wants of others. You will need to find a way to impact others with your experience, skills, or knowledge. It isn't enough to have a talent, gift or passion; you must master it and bring it to the marketplace to serve others. You will also need your passion to fuel you when things get rough. Success comes to those who are willing to keep hustling, despite adversities, distractions, and challenges. Also, keep in mind, the greatest rewards come when you give of yourself!

CONCLUSION

If you need a fresh dose of hustle now and then and business tips along the way, my video podcast show, *Hustle & Heart TV*, gives entrepreneurs, small business owners, dreamers, and developers just like you a weekly dose of inspiration and important business-building information.

I started this video podcast for a few reasons and with a new "why." First, I wanted to grow my brand, influence, and income. I have been able to significantly increase my email list, establish nine additional streams of income, and develop a platform to coach and teach people about video podcasting from one passion and one purpose. Video podcasting is an incredible way to grow your business, by the way. If you're not promoting your business through a podcast or video podcast, you are missing a title wave of opportunity!

Second, I wanted to show more people how podcasting can help grow their business. You can create a show around just about any topic or message. You can have a show about fur balls or designer doodads. Trust me, the weirder the better. There are countless industries, professions, and areas of interest that make for great podcast shows. I'm happy to help you develop some ideas. Or if you have a show, I can help you incorporate ways to market and monetize it. You can reach me by email at info@DariethChisolm.com or visit my website at www.DariethChisolm.com to learn about all of the ways I'm helping people build their brand, influence, and income through podcasting and coaching.

Third, I was looking for a new challenge and a new way to express myself. So with the wave of podcasting and the spring board of opportunities it offers, it was an enticing adventure to begin.

My "why"? To give back in a significant way to other entrepreneurs. When I'm interviewing other successful people and sharing their inspiration and important information, I feel like I'm providing value and resources that are vital for success in business. My video podcast show is always available to watch and listen to and is a resource for people to turn to get practical advice from movers and shakers.

It's the perfect intersection for me.

But I can tell you, this almost didn't happen, simply because I got a little fearful about launching a video podcast.

Why? I was about to let the fear of having no experience with creating and producing something brand new, that I knew nothing about, stop me. Then I remembered— I only needed to employ a few of the ten strategies that highly successful entrepreneurs use and practice.

First, I needed a new *"why."* I knew it was important to create a show like *Hustle & Heart TV* to bridge all the things that I am most passionate about: business, the successful mindset, entrepreneurship, personal development, and goal setting. I wanted to do it in a format that I was most comfortable with: being on camera. I knew I wanted to tell the stories that inspire others, to give back, and to give value to the marketplace. I was prepared to do something that is trending as one of the most popular ways to market yourself and your business.

I found my perfect intersection, and I wanted to dive deeply into creating it.

Then I needed to determine *my goals*. What would the video podcast look like? How would it be perceived in the marketplace? Who would I interview? What kind of money did I want to earn? Where would I find the guests? What types of advertisers did I want to have on the show? How many shows did I want to pump out? I just needed to put a pen to paper to develop my goals and post them on my big bulletin board and stay focused on them. I began to measure, monitor, adjust, and control as needed.

I needed to be fearless and not afraid to fail. I needed to put myself out there in spite of the possibility of failure and go after it. I needed to know that failure was certainly a possibility but so was success, and that doing this was truly challenging me to learn, grow and expand, and experience new things.

As I became braver and more committed to reaching my goals and understanding my "why," I knew I needed to put together *a team and systems*. It would be impossible to make this happen on my own…not with all of the other balls that I have moving in the air.

I'm fortunate to always have the support of my husband, Dr. Arnold Tarpley, an amazing and talented podiatrist, and my incredible son, Tre. But I needed more manpower—no, woman power. So I'm blessed and quite fortunate to have an amazing assistant, Kelly Frost. She has watched me impregnate this idea, carry it, have labor, birth it, and now watch it crawl into existence. I also needed a team of photographers and editors, especially since the first batch of interns quit on the day they were to show up to shoot and edit. I'm now blessed with an incredible team of videographers and additional apprentices and assistance. They are all eager to earn this experience and craft something new and exciting.

I get up every day with a mission to accomplish my goals—driven by my "why" and my passion, being unafraid, unapologetic, connected with my team and my systems, and ready to hustle.

I truly believe that is part of the reason why I can celebrate the early successes that we've had. I'm enjoying subscribers and downloads from all over the world—places like Zimbabwe, Kuwait, Japan, the Netherlands, and more.

If I hadn't taken this chance to totally engage my passion and run relentlessly toward another venture, I wouldn't be enjoying this success.

My hustle now consists of success coaching, speaking and training, podcasting, and teaching other's how to start their own podcast shows. I am now living my new purpose, showing others how to unleash their passion, how to turn it into profit, and love their journey.

I'm telling you, you can't even imagine what awaits you if you just hold out and persevere! That next best thing could be right around the corner, if you'll only take one more step, trust, and believe. Stay focused on your dream and centered in your passion. Do whatever it takes to chase your desires. It is up to you to keep striving and serving the highest purpose for your talents and gifts. It's up to you to *hustle* until you make something happen, because action creates momentum, which creates unanticipated opportunities and positive results.

The world is waiting for you to unleash your passion.

ACTION PLAN

Now that you've come to the end of the book, the true hustle begins. I recommend that you go back and review your answers from Chapters One through Nine and each of your Action Plans. Create a notebook that contains all of your answered questions, a vision board, dreams, goals, etc., and keep it handy for those days when you need to be anchored again to your "why."

Now go get your hustle on! *Now* is the time to unleash your passions!

HUSTLE TIP

"We all have the same 24 hours but you absolutely have to view yours in a different way, if you have to fill orders at 5 o'clock in the morning or you have to fill them at midnight than that's what you have to do, and hopefully you are doing it with pleasure and you're doing it knowing that it's for the greater good. It's hard, you're tired, but people don't get ahead sitting on the couch flicking channels, it is enticing but you just don't."

- Nicole Narvaez Manns, Founder/Owner/ Inventor of Nikki's Magic Wand - *Hustle & Heart TV* on Episode 24

HEART TIP

"One thing that is extremely important is being thankful and giving back from the very first wand that I have ever sent in the mail, I have sent a hand written thank you note and I do to this day. Every single order, I write a hand written note and thank people for their order. So I'm grateful, I'm thankful, I just bought thank you cards that say without you, there is no us and I believe that and we give back."

- Nicole Narvaez Manns, Founder/Owner/Inventor of Nikki's Magic Wand - *Hustle & Heart TV* on Episode 24

RESOURCES

HUSTLE HACKS TO GO

A hustle hack a day keeps prosperity coming your way!

Directions: I have compiled 21 days of Hustle Hacks to keep you moving in the right direction after reading the book. Read one a day to keep prosperity coming your way. When you get to the end, start over again!

DAY ONE

Our Hustle Hack for Day One comes from Rob Wilson – personal finance expert, speaker, and financial advisor who was a guest on *Hustle & Heart TV*, Episode 7.

Here's Rob...

"I think we are in a fantastic period of existence and I'm trying to take advantage of it as much as I can...

"No matter how many followers, friends, or how many views you have, nobody cares about you. Really, people don't care. The only thing they care about right now is if you can help them, and it really doesn't matter—all those other things you have...

"If they feel like you have something that can help them get what they want, then you're 95 percent done at that point...

"In general I think that careers are largely gone. I think everybody has his or her own business right now regardless if you're sorta working and you get a paycheck from somebody else—you're still your own business, in my opinion. If you're going to run your own business, you gotta be comfortable selling, and a lot of people feel like the word 'sell' is a [dirty] four-letter word. And I get that, because you don't get taught how to sell when you're coming up in high school or any kind of school. You go through school in order to become a good employee. That's the model that we have here, at least in this country. It takes hard work to try to de-program something that's been programmed into you for eighteen to twenty years. But 'sell' is not a four-letter word; if you're working for an employer, you've gotta sell yourself. If you're working in an MLM, you've got to be able to see a product...

"You just have to have more activity. You have to keep doing it over and over and over and over again, and eventually you get better at it. And the fact that you keep doing it over and over again [means] you're going to be better than 90 percent of the other people, because they're going to quit, and they won't even be there anyway...

"The best investment you can ever make is in yourself, because the returns on that are infinite. You don't have to pay for yourself; you're already there, so the returns are fantastic. So anything that you hope to grow or build, you've got to put money into it. You've got to spend money on equipment, you've got to spend money getting trained, or whatever it is. If you don't think you're a good salesman, go take a course, go have somebody train you, go get a mentor that you might have to pay. But get something that's going to take you to the next level. If you're not willing to invest in yourself, why would anybody else invest in your business...?

"I am actively trying to get better, and you have got to be willing to suck at the beginning. And that's just it: you have got to let go of your ego...

"So the first product that you put out, if it's not bad, if you're not embarrassed about it, you probably waited too long to launch it. So be willing to be bad but get better, learn from your mistakes, and eventually it's going to come...

"Am I going to be physically hurt? If I'm not, let's just go do it to see what happens...

"There has *never*, ever, in the history of the world, been an easier, better time to start or launch a business. The Internet has leveled the playing field for everyone, and to not take advantage of that just because you feel like you might get your feelings hurt at some point is just heartbreaking to me...

"You can't lead by fear. If people are afraid of you or [of] losing their job, you will never, ever get the best performance out of them if you're leading by fear. But if you empower people— and you may have to build people up so much that they leave you, that they go off and they go on to bigger, better things—I would say that if you're a leader, that's the best possible job that you can ever do...

"You hear financial advisors and people say that the key to it is just to live within your means. That's the worst, absolute worst, financial advice by far that I ever heard in my life, because who is somebody else to tell you what your means are? By saying that, you are inherently telling somebody, 'I don't think that you could do much better than that...'"

DAY TWO

Our Hustle Hack for Day Two comes from Sabrina Saunders – Pittsburgh Executive Director, Strong Women, Strong Girls who was a guest on *Hustle & Heart TV*, Episode 14.

Here's Sabrina…

"I have a small team, and we are a *team*. We work together to make sure every aspect of the organization is seen through [to the end,] and that's what it takes. It takes dedication and commitment, and for me the newness of it is keeping it exciting and fun…

"I feel like I got a glimpse of what it would be like to lead, and I never let it go, and it is that excitement that keeps me going…

"Hit that next milestone, and reach that next goal, and that continues to stir my soul…!

"Following through and following up are things that have been instrumental in my success—making sure that the connections are made. Pittsburgh is a great place, full of opportunity for young people, and I have been able to make connections by networking and going to events. And some of this is very tiresome. It's consistently working at it, and consistently being out and selling yourself and what you can do, and making sure that you're not the only person that knows what you're capable of…

"Be prepared to work hard, and recognize that it's worth it in the end and that there's no sacrifice—it's all opportunity. And even the things that seem hard and harsh are all opportunity for something better...

"Anything that involves helping other people has some strain and strife, and it's going to sometimes get tough, and it can get very lonely. Individuals will say it's lonely at the top; well, in the non-profit world, there are lots of organizations and lots of leadership, but it can be very lonely...

"When you prepare yourself, you insert yourself into situations that you cannot be removed from...

"As long as you take that first step, you start to see yourself in every reality that you've painted... Until it's real to you, it's never going to happen. Taking that first step is so important in getting it done...

"If I've made just one huge mistake a week, I've done a good job, I feel, and that's ok, as long as you're learning from them and not making those mistakes again...

"I think that you have to explore your interest, you have to find if something is for you by doing. You're not going to learn by sitting and watching—you have to get out there and explore and do the things you feel you may be interested in, and get involved in some way..."

DAY THREE

Our Hustle Hack for Day Three comes from Karin Mayr – CEO & founder, Sabika Jewelry who was our guest on *Hustle & Heart TV*, Episode 2.

Here's Karin...

"I knew if I would keep going and if I would get over my own fears and over myself—and I understand I would have [these fears] on a daily basis, but I would overcome them—I would see where it would take me. I didn't know where it would take me, but I knew it would take me somewhere...

"I don't overcome fear. I don't even try to overcome fear. I don't strive to overcome fear. I embrace fear as part of everybody's life, including my own...

"Something I'm very grateful for: I know what my shortcomings are, and I'm never too proud to ask people to help me when I'm stuck...

"In my world I don't have to have the biggest world, Sabika world. I don't care how big it will be. I want it to be a world where everybody has equal value and where big goals or small goals only make a difference for the individual but not for us as a company...

"I always like to under-promise and over-deliver. I would always rather have a positive surprise than a disappointment..."

DAY FOUR

Our Hustle Hack for Day Four comes from Pat McDonnell – CEO & owner, Restaurant Holdings; owner, Atria's, Ditka's restaurants, Juniper Grill, who was our guest on *Hustle & Heart TV*, Episode 13.

Here's Pat...

"You have to love what you do... How do you deal with adversity? It's easy to deal with things when they are going good. You've got to persevere. You've got to be confident. You've got to let your employees know that things are going to be okay and that you're strong and you're going to make it...

"So many times physical fitness is a way of life. If you are physically fit, then you are able to be mentally fit, in my opinion...

"Marketing is menu development and engineering and refreshing of the buildings...keeping them fresh and evolving and not staying the same...

"Anytime you get someone to invest with you and be partners with you, it makes a difference. We ask that the proprietors live in the neighborhood... You're the face of the restaurant, and it's important [for you] to be there. And I think that is key to success, to be in the neighborhood and to have what I call 'skin in the game,' you make an investment, and that investment is meant to pay off for you. It's a different level of commitment and our people like it, too...

"You hear that in corporate all the time, that it's just not warm and fuzzy…you feel like a number and you're not part of the team. I think a lot of other companies lose that culture, and they think more about the bottom line. They get away from really what's driving their business, and it's the people as much as anything…

"I always say I want raving employees because that will create raving fans. If your employees are happy and they come to work and they want to be there, that is such a difference—that's the edge…

"It starts with people, and nowadays if you don't have good food, you aren't going to be in business, so good food is a given. But what you do from there is create an experience. I think that's the most important thing for anyone in the business…

"It's all about culture and training and having people that want to be there. We all carry our burdens when we walk through the door coming into our place of work; we have things on our mind, whatever it may be; just life's opportunities. People come to our restaurant to take an hour or hour and a half to forget about those things, and it's our job to take it off their shoulders and allow them to experience an hour and a half of peace…

"Being well capitalized is important. Don't start a project until you have the right capital…"

DAY FIVE

Our Hustle Hack for Day Five comes from Ray Higdon

– author, speaker, network marketer; founder, Team Start Living who was our guest on *Hustle & Heart TV*, Episode 9.

Here's Ray...

"Leverage creates freedom...

"The four most important things for me, and what I suggest that people look at, is community, support, training, and leadership. Those four things are the most important, in my opinion, because they will help to grow you and help you to learn the right way to do this profession...

"The number one stumbling block of new network marketers is they come into this profession and seek acceptance and approval—and you ain't gonna get it with everyone. So this is the deal: you gotta be focused on where you want to go...

"Fear is always the barrier to breakthrough...

"I'm just not addicted to the outcome. Even the best of the best are only going to close 20-30 percent, and you just gotta realize that...

"The lessons are [that] you can create anything from wherever you are, and you just gotta let go of all the reasons that you're using to justify where you are and instead say 'here's where I wanna go...'

"I believe in personal branding. I believe in *you* being a unit of value in your marketplace...

"There's no limitation to who you can help. And why would I just help people in my team if my mission is to raise the level of the entire profession? I think that we can raise the level of this entire profession by doing great training...so that when my teammates go to talk to somebody, they haven't been negatively affected by people in other companies...

"Invest, learn, and teach..."

DAY SIX
Our Hustle Hack for Day Six comes from Denise Walsh
– author; speaker; network marketer, It Works! Global who was our guest on *Hustle & Heart TV*, Episode 5.

Here's Denise...

"The biggest thing to learn is to keep your mouth shut, because when you do, you'll find so much can happen. But we often puke. We call it puking, where we spew and projectile vomit and try to look taller than we are by knowing all these big words and end up making a disconnection rather than the connection we are looking for. So listening is an important leader skill...

"When you have a community where people are positive and they're pouring positive energy into each other, most people don't want to leave...

"If I'd let those no's stop me at first, I wouldn't be here, where I am today. For getting through those first few no's [there has to be] an understanding; it's just a piece of the business, and it doesn't mean anything negative on your part. And then alongside that is belief, belief in yourself, belief in the company, belief in the product, and when you can achieve complete belief—and from the bottom of your heart—that this is where you're supposed to be. Then those no's don't matter...

"Sometimes we let fear stop us, and fear gets in the way before we even get started. But the only way to conquer fear is to take action. So even if you're scared, even if you're nervous, even if you know you have a little bit of worry, do it anyway, because the more you do it, the more confident you'll become...

"I don't work my business based on how I feel, I work my business on what I want...

"There's two days in this business: the day you decide to join and the day you decide to work..."

DAY SEVEN

Our Hustle Hack for Day Seven comes from Nicole Cooper – Internet marketer, speaker who was our guest on *Hustle & Heart TV*, Episode 16.

Here's Nicole...

"I believe in leveraging other people's systems, money, resources, tools, talents, and stories...

"L.I.S.T.: You *learn* something, you *implement* what you just learned, you *share* what you just learned, and you turn around and *teach* what you just learned. Whenever I learned something, I took action on it. When I took action on it, I distributed it and syndicated it. Once I syndicated it and got results, I took those results and I taught how I just got those results based on what I just did...

"When it comes to Internet marketing, what most people don't understand about making money online is that it's pretty much you connecting with an audience who, number one, they like you, and number two, they see something that you have that they desire, and number three, they are willing to exchange money with you for it...

"When you first get started in this process, you don't want to feel like you have to know everything. Approach it from a *look over my shoulder* point of view...

"I don't want people to feel like they have to be the expert before they can take action. The more you can give that over-the-shoulder approach, the warmer it is to your audience because they can relate, and you're able to immediately connect with them in a way where you understand where they're at...

"You can be an entrepreneur or an intrepreneur...what that means is that you can work for yourself, or you can take your skills and work for someone else...

"If someone presents you with an opportunity, say yes first and figure out how to do it later...

"It takes ten years to be an overnight success...

"My story has become my brand, my platform, my business model...

"I'm so adamant about reading because books are my mentors. A lot of times many of us look at life and we say, 'I don't have anyone around to help me.' If I need to know anything, I can just reference a book...

"If you want to know where your heart is and where you put your treasure, check your bank account. Where does your money go...?

"I want to die empty; I don't want an ounce of potential left in me."

DAY EIGHT

Our Hustle Hack for Day Eight comes from Stephanie Donegan – Executive Leadership Coach, author who was our guest on *Hustle & Heart TV*, Episode 6.

Here's Stephanie...

"I am the client magnet specialist. I help entrepreneurs just like you create irresistibly juicy marketing strategies to attract your ideal, high-paying clients. A huge part of embracing my title is mindset. A huge part of this is wealth consciousness and a lot of training. I'm really big on that but actually don't lead with that. I'll lead with becoming irresistibly juicy. Why? Because most people don't answer the call of 'Do you have a screwed-up mindset? If so, call me.' Most people don't think their mindset is completely wrong...

"More [often] than not, people can do the right steps, but they're over here in fear and they're over here in doubt and they're over here really saying, 'What if I fail, and what if this happens and what if that happens...?' It's blocking them from the success they need...

"A huge part of becoming irresistibly juicy is finding your place in the world...

"Don't work with people you don't like...

"We're creating success; we don't have time for passiveness...

"Don't just go into coaching because it's the fastest growing industry or because of the amount of money you can make. Go into it because you really want to change lives...

"You need to create nonnegotiables...

"How can you expect others to invest in you when you won't invest in you...?

"If you don't love where you are, wherever you are in the journey, you can't get the next best thing...

"You have to be grateful for exactly what it is you have, whether it is two clients or twenty clients, because if you are not grateful for these two, the twenty won't come..."

DAY NINE

Our Hustle Hack for Day Nine comes from Elisabet Rodriquez Dennehy – author; speaker; owner, Rodriguez and Associates, LLC who was our guest on *Hustle & Heart TV*, Episode 3.

Here's Elisabet...

"Reframing and shifting is about doing two things: staying true to yourself and then understand that there are a couple of things you need to just shift, move, enhance, or reduce. Sometimes we are too shy, too quiet, too complacent, or too nice in the corporate environment. In the corporate environment, we have to understand that we have to be elegant. We also have to understand that we have to be assertive. That's an example of a shift—that I be and continue to be agreeable and nice and personable, but at the same time understand that we have to find ways in which our body language, our voice, our demeanor, the way we express ourselves, the way we interact with other people, we also remain assertive...

"I cannot influence people if I'm faking it, if I'm not being fully myself, if I'm not fully present in front of you...

"Behavior change requires repetition...

"If you don't get the job, two things need to happen. You need to understand, 'What will I need to do for my next round?' But most importantly, if a friend, especially a girlfriend, a women professional, got that position, support her 150 percent...

"When one of us wins, we all win...

"Don't become a little bit of everything for everyone...you want to be known for what you do best...

"Don't forget the day you woke up and said, 'This is what I want to do, this is going to be my passion, this is what I'm going to grow, this particular service or product or skill. This is what my strength is!' Then there is no competition, because I'm not trying to be everything to everyone. I am who I am, and I can give you just this. Oh, but when I do, I can guarantee you're going to be satisfied. That is the recipe for entrepreneurs, men and women, but most importantly, I think, for women...

"Books are my friends...I learn through reading...

"I was not this clear when I was thirty. I was not this clear when I was forty. I always say the best decade of my life was my fifties, [but] I'm enjoying my sixties immensely..."

DAY TEN

Our Hustle Hack for Day Ten comes from Troy Miles – owner, The Miles Group, Lincoln Heritage Life Insurance Company who was our guest on *Hustle & Heart TV*, Episode 1.

Here's Troy...

"I saw it. It made sense to me, and if it makes sense to me, it makes dollars...

"You are in charge of your own paycheck...if you are in charge of your own income, you're in charge of your own life...

"Faith and positive energy, that's the key. You have to believe in what you're doing. We go after the people who believe in us, believe in themselves, and they believe in what we're doing, and that's the people that we go after...

"It's really simple for them, because it's all about positive energy. We don't deal with negative people or back stabbers or people who are just out for themselves—we go after people who want to achieve greatness. We look for leaders. We want people to grow. We want that person who doesn't just want to be a writer, even though that's okay, but we look for people who want to go to that next level. We want people that want to go to that next level real soon...

"As a leader, I have no fear; I have no fear of failing. I know if I screw up on something, I'm okay with saying, 'You know what, I screwed up and now I know that doesn't work...'

"Do not push the boulder up the hill. Push the boulder down the hill and run behind it...

"You have to take the stairs, not the elevator. There is no quick way to the top. You have to be willing to put in the time..."

DAY ELEVEN
Our Hustle Hack for Day Eleven comes from Collin Stover – magician and mentalist who was our guest on *Hustle & Heart TV*, Episode 10.

Here's Collin...

"A lot of entrepreneurs and business owners, when they are first starting out, worry a lot about creating the perfect thing and planning and planning and planning, and they never execute. But I think it's so important to know when to say enough is enough. There is a quote by Dan Kennedy, and he says, 'Good is good enough...'

"I'm a huge believer in getting a minimum viable product or service—spending the least amount of money, spending the least amount of time on something just to get something together, just a sample, and putting it out there and seeing the response. Because if no one responds, then you just saved yourself a lot of time and money. If a lot of people respond, then you can make it perfect and you can fine tune it. I think it is very important to make that decision to go for it and not stall...

"Perfection is not a good thing. If you reach perfection that means that you are not growing anymore...

"I also have a couple mentors that I follow, which I think is very important, obviously, to have in all areas in your life...

"I try not to focus on learning too many new things all the time. I have my core ten to fifteen things that I do all the time, and really it burns down to about three things I do over and over and over again. I'd rather be the best at those three tricks, than be average at a thousand things...

"Systems are extremely important, and most of my systems come into play on the marketing end of things. I have a twenty-step system...and it does one of two things: One, it's quality control to make sure I don't forget about anything and that everyone is getting the same experience; two, if I ever decide to hire someone someday and stop performing someday and rent out my brand, I can just hand them that checklist. I don't have to do anything. I don't have to explain anything. I don't have to pull my hair out wondering, 'Why aren't you getting this?', because I have a checklist, and it's easy, and it's written in a language that anyone can understand, not just language that I can understand...

"I learned that I had a lot to learn about service. I was great at magic, but I had a lot to learn about service. So now I have revolved my entire business around service. I guarantee that I give the best service out of any entertainer that anybody's ever had..."

DAY TWELVE

Our Hustle Hack for Day Twelve comes from LaShanda Henry – website designer, internet marketer; founder of SistaSense.com, who was our guest on *Hustle & Heart TV*, Episode 12.

Here's LaShanda...

"In order for you to create a successful business, you have to be self-motivated. So if there are things other than just the business that are blocking you, then someone like Lucinda is really good at helping women activate and get clear...

"Whether you come to me with a startup, restart, or [are in] a jump start phase, there is somebody in the community that can help you...

"Before you get online, get offline. It's all about clarity for me. Because as you know, it's all about social media, and everybody is like, 'Do this and do this!' But, before you do that, what do you want to accomplish? Find the platform that best fits your personality. I was a typer and not a talker, so blogging always worked best for me...

"I believe in having a personal brain dump where I basically say, get that pen and that pad and write down all the things that you actually want to accomplish right now. But then start with the ones that are realistic for you, and honestly, that's what I did...

"There are so many low cost, nominal tools, like WordPress and PayPal, for doing voice messaging. I always love doing

Speed Pipe on my web site. Keep in mind, what do you need? Because you may see that there are all these different web tools, and they may look all wonderful and great, but if you don't need it, don't add it to your space. Just focus on those things that you really need right now...

"The challenge of working from home is just simply to continue to self-motivate, because you don't have somebody telling you this is what you need to do every day...

"Whatever I learn, I teach...

"If you've got an iPad or any mobile device, turn the cellular data off, strategically, so that there are no pings, no tweets, no Facebook or Google alerts, so that you are not distracted all the time...

"When you have a 9-5 and you're trying to build your business, you have to be very careful that you're spending your 9-5 money back into the business...

"When it comes to clarity, it takes years, and it's really important to figure out whether or not you need to change direction, or if you've got to dig deep and figure out how to make what you're doing work better for you...

"Find a platform and do it consistently so that you can be known for being on that space on a regular basis. Every leader has to have a following, and you basically have to have a clear location as to where your following is going to congregate. I think that is a big part of the process...

"Get a collection of mentors around you. It takes a while to get physical mentors..."

DAY THIRTEEN

Our Hustle Hack for Day Thirteen comes from Sam Deep – author and executive leadership coach, Sam Deep Leadership Academy, who was our guest on *Hustle & Heart TV*, Episode 8.

Here's Sam...

"I think leaders really do two things. More than anything else, the first thing they do is that they engage people, they win their hearts. The second thing they do, and this is the toughest, is that they hold their feet to the fire. They make sure that people are accountable for their performance and for their outcomes in service...

"[Show your people you are] putting yourself in second place [and] putting your people in first place. So what that says is this: You can really focus on listening to them. You're going to go out of your way to show your appreciation for them. You're going to see yourself as their champion. You're going to see yourself as a person who goes to bat for them, that defends them, that brings the resources to them that they need to do their work. The other thing that so many leaders find out for the first time when they study servant-leadership is that you need to ask them what they need from you...

"Understand that they'll be more successful if they're more able to influence the other people that they need to work with...

"You can't let people think that 'the way I succeed is by outdoing that other person,' but 'the way I succeed is by outdoing myself...'

"Too often people don't set goals. What they do is set actions...

"We have to make a commitment to sitting down at least quarterly in reviewing the goals, because sometimes the goals become not appropriate anymore in the world, because it is always changing...

"Here is really the key: I have to know that at the end of the year, there's going to be consequences either having met or not my goals. Positive consequences if I've met my goal and negative consequences if I've not met my goal. There's going to be some pain if I don't achieve my goals..."

DAY FOURTEEN

Our Hustle Hack for Day Fourteen comes from Charlie Batch – former NFL quarterback/Pittsburgh Steelers, and founder of Best of the Batch Foundation, who was our guest on *Hustle & Heart TV*, Episode 4.

Here's Charlie...

"Everyone is different. Number one: It starts with passion... it's something that you have to continue to grind, because there may be a lot of 'no's' when you're going through it...

"No matter what your mission statement is, you don't want to have any mission drifters. Meaning, you started out with this, but now we are going to add this element into it, and it takes away what the original meaning and original foundation was supposed to look like...

"Football doesn't go on forever, and it's important to let people know who you are behind the helmet..."

DAY FIFTEEN

Our Hustle Hack for Day Fifteen comes from Rob Furman, Elementary Principal and National Presenter for Furman Educational Resources, who was our guest on *Hustle & Heart TV*, Episode 11.

Here's Rob...

"You have to have your nose in the books, you've got to stay current on research. You need to look beyond tomorrow and to be looking well into the future. Things change, and are changing so quickly in our society... 'We are teaching children to have jobs that haven't yet even been created, using technology that hasn't yet been discovered, to solve problems that we haven't even thought of yet', what a daunting task...

"In order to do that, we need to be able to think into the future and any businessman, and leader needs to be able to think 10, or 15 years down the road because those changes are starting now...

"Follow your passion if you feel like you want to do something, and you've got to do it. Take no prisoners, I love to say that, you need to just go and nothing gets in your way and with that type of passion, anything can happen."

DAY SIXTEEN

Our Hustle Hack for Day Sixteen comes from Roberto Clemente Jr., President and CEO of RCJ Global Impact, LLC and Former Professional Baseball Player who was our guest on *Hustle & Heart TV*, Episode 11.

Here's Roberto...

"If you don't like what you do and you wake up in the morning and you don't like your job, get out! Go and find a good job, look around you and ask what do you do, you'll find it, you might be sitting next to a person that actually maybe looking for someone that can give you a job. A better thing to do is to find a job that when you wake up in the morning you are happy about your job and your business."

DAY SEVENTEEN

Our Hustle Hack for Day Seventeen comes from Candi Castleberry-Singleton, Chief Inclusion and Diversity Officer at UPMC, who was our guest on *Hustle & Heart TV*, Episode 18.

Here's Candi...

"Love what you do, the reason I have the capacity is because I love what I do...when you love what you it doesn't feel like work...

"Find somebody who loves you and can remind you who you are."

DAY EIGHTEEN

Our Hustle Hack for Day Eighteen comes from Mame Kendall, Owner of Smoke Cigar Smoke Cigar Shop & Lounge Inc., who was our guest on *Hustle & Heart TV*, Episode 20.

Here's Mame...

"Don't ever give up, just keep going, you have to make it happen, it doesn't matter if you are on two hours of sleep or no sleep you have got to make it happen because if you don't, someone else will...

"Don't forget where you came from, don't forget your family, that's the most important thing to me, I have a very small family and I'm very thankful for the family that I do have."

DAY NINETEEN

Our Hustle Hack for Day Nineteen comes from Shellie Hipsky, Associate Professor at Robert Morris Univeristy, Author, and Speaker, who was our guest on *Hustle & Heart TV*, Episode 21.

Here's Shellie...

"You gotta go big or go home, you have to be able to envision as big as you can and go for it, find it, manifest it, make it happen...

"Be true to yourself, be true to who you are, what do you bring to the table and then go out there and show the world."

DAY TWENTY

Our Hustle Hack for Day Twenty comes from Rebecca Harris, Director at the Center for Women's Entrepreneurship at Chatham University, who was our guest on *Hustle & Heart TV*, Episode 22.

Here's Rebecca...

"I don't work just 8 or 9 hours days, I work all the time. I work mornings and evenings, I work a lot on the weekends. You can't have a finite time and think, well that's all that I can do. You have to be hustling all the time...

"It's passion, I don't know how I could do my work if I wasn't passionate about it and so if you really aren't passionate about your work you have 3 choices: Stay and accept, stay in and change it, or you exit but make sure you are passionate."

DAY TWENTY ONE
Our Hustle Hack for Day Twenty One comes from Kiya Tomlin, Fashion Designer at Uptown Sweats by Kiya Tomlin, who was our guest on *Hustle & Heart TV*, Episode 23.

Here's Kiya...

"Find what you love to do and find a way to make money doing it...

"I am a perfectionist at heart, but you can be a perfectionist to the point of paralysis and so I just have to realize that it's okay to say this is it, this is good for now, move on, let's see what happens and then improve from there...

"I think of everything as a work in progress and it's part of the journey and it will get better over time and each piece that I create may not be the perfect piece that I had envisioned but there is another life to it that can come after and I take that into all aspects of my life which allows me to balance to be the mom and the wife as well as the career woman...

"I look for people that understand my vision and what I'm trying to do, understand where I'm trying to take it and my brand and what it means and is also excited about it...

"Get out there, learn, and get hands on experience anyway that you can. Read, research, and learn about all of the various aspects of the business. You don't need to do all of them but to have some background information on them and then to find the kind of people that can help you with those areas that you don't want to do...

"You can't achieve perfection, you're going to end up waiting, you have to jump in and swim and by doing that you'll be exposed to other experiences and opportunities, learn from your choices and really to consider them choices and I think we are so afraid of making choices that will make life uncomfortable for us. But I see it as, our choices really just dictate experiences that we learn from and grow from."

Watch *Hustle & Heart TV with Darieth Chisolm:*

www.HustleandHeartTV.com

Subscribe and download on:
iTunes
Stitcher Radio
YouTube

Make podcasting, video podcasting and
video blogging part of your success.

Get the tools and the support you need to
launch a successful podcast at
www.ThePodcastersAcademy.com

Contact Darieth for individual, private and group coaching at
www.DariethChisolm.com/Coaching

CONNECT WITH DARIETH CHISOLM

www.DariethChisolm.com

www.facebook.com/dariethchisolm

www.twitter.com/DariethChisolm

www.youtube.com/user/Cinnamon9292

www.linkedin.com/pub/darieth-chisolm

5:30
Paenmo / Brooklyn

9 PM.
Sunset
12 PM
Ram.